Estate Planning Success® for Women

Professor Lynne Marie Kohm, J.D.
Attorney Mark L. James, M.B.A., J.D., LL.M. (tax)

Estate Planning Success® for Women

9 SIMPLE STEPS *to* PLAN YOUR ESTATE *with* FORESIGHT, CLARITY *and* THOUGHTFULNESS *for* THE BENEFIT OF THOSE YOU LOVE

PUBLISHING CO.
Barron Publishing Co.
State College, Pennsylvania

For updates on the material in this book, visit www.barronpublishing.com.

Estate Planning Success® for Women

Copyright © 2005 by Lynne Marie Kohm and Mark L. James

Published by

Barron Publishing Co.
Post Office Box 532
State College, PA 16804
(800) 748-0399
www.barronpublishing.com

PRINTED IN THE UNITED STATES OF AMERICA
Cover Design: George Foster
Interior Design: Christopher Davis
Editor: Sherry Sullivan

ISBN: 0-9716376-4-4

Warning and Disclaimer

A Note about the Glossary

Throughout this book you will see words and phrases in small caps when they are first introduced. These terms are listed in the Glossary.

Estate Planning Success® for Women
9 Simple Steps to Plan Your Estate with Foresight, Clarity and Thoughtfulness for the Benefit of Those You Love

Table of Contents

Preface

*W*e want to help you avoid the trauma and hard feelings that we have seen many families suffer because of the failure to plan. We have seen heirs endure lawsuits and families devastated when they learn that their loved one was already incompetent and not able to sign a power of attorney to avoid a guardianship hearing. And, we have seen the look on executors' faces as they sign checks made out to the Internal Revenue Service for hundreds of thousands of dollars in payment of the federal estate tax. We have been involved in fixing what goes wrong due to the failure to plan, and it is our sincere desire that this book will help you plan your estate to avoid future problems.

The purpose of this book is to present the world of estate planning in the most practical and understandable terms possible. More specifically, this book is designed to allow you to read targeted chapters that pertain to your individual needs as a woman. Each chapter addresses particular estate planning strategies related to your season in life and your needs. Ultimately, of course, you will need assistance from experienced estate planning advisors to work out the options and strategies for your own situation.

Estate Planning Success® for Women has been researched exhaustively, and the contents have been honed into a reference guide for women and their loved ones. It unravels the complex world of estate planning in the context of the multifaceted lives of women. Capturing the essence of the unique issues women face, it explains simple steps to plan with insight and precision, to benefit those you love and to save money and stay in control of your assets in any circumstances. Whether you are widowed, married, single, divorced, retired or planning for retirement, a business owner or professional person, just entering the work force, or just want to learn the best ways to protect your estate, this book will save you significant time and money. From probate and inheritance taxes to living trusts, this book covers every estate planning issue necessary to keep you on track in planning your estate. It will help you to plan your estate with foresight, clarity and thoughtfulness for the benefit of those you love.

Step 1

Understand Why Women are Unique

Topics Include

Women's Lives, Wants and Needs

Financial Security

Retirement Planning

Important Questions

Family Legacy

Introduction

A BEAUTIFUL BOUQUET OF FLOWERS captures the gaze of a woman who was given this array by her husband and children. What was the occasion? She sat all day in chaotic Atlanta Hartsfield airport for them. Having learned 15 minutes before their flight was leaving that the children's brand new personalized baseball bats could not be carried onto the flight for security reasons, and knowing the importance of her husband getting back to his office after a family vacation, without another thought she realized that she must take these precious items back through airport security and check them as baggage on a later flight. It meant she would miss the flight with her family. It also meant that she had to risk a standby reservation on a flight sometime within the following 24 hours. But that is just what she needed to do to put her family first. She considered it a small sacrifice of love. That's just what women do, isn't it?

Women's Lives Are Unique

That's why this book is so important. Women live most of their lives centered on others. Whether children, husbands, parents, ex-husbands, or stepchildren, most women by nature care for the people in their lives in a sacrificial way. This book understands this caregiver nature and challenges women to consider how to care for themselves while also leaving a legacy for those whom they love.

Women also appreciate having peace of mind. Being assured that your loved ones will have that same peace of mind at your death is important. The more you plan now, the less they have to be concerned about later. This foresight also decreases family strife and interpersonal battles that may arise upon the death of a family member.

While estate planning is the same for men and women, there are special considerations for women. Married, single, widowed or divorced, a little estate planning done in advance can prevent a myriad of problems later on.

Women Are Different From Men

Most estate planning volumes are written by men, for men, with men as the standard. It is important to remember, however, that men and women are different. Men and women tend to think differently, live differently, earn differently, spend differently and save differently. Women are just not men. They are unique in many ways.

Foremost, women tend to outlive men by an average of seven years. That means that one day, whether you are single, married, divorced or widowed, the odds are that as a woman, you will be the sole financial planner and decision maker. You will likely live at least a few years without the support of a spouse near the end of your life, if not sooner.

In fact, 50 percent of all women older than 65 are widows, and widows frequently suffer a sharp drop in their standard of living. Women over 65 are three times as likely as men to be widowed. According to the United States Accounting Office, three-quarters of all elderly persons living below the poverty line are women. These are powerful reasons why women need to participate in all areas of their financial and estate planning now.

Women Must Plan for Their Own Financial Security

Historically, many women married for financial security, but today the majority of women will spend nearly one-third of their adult lives financially on their own. Ninety-nine percent of household decisions are made by women, and a great many of those decisions are financial in nature. According to the United States Census Bureau, 90 percent of all American women will have to bear the responsibility for their own financial security. But this need is complicated by the facts of women's lives.

Women typically earn less than men and spend less time in the workforce. In 2003, women in the United States earned 72 cents for every dollar earned by men. Women earn less money and work fewer years on the average than men, generally due to family priorities. Women also change jobs more often than men for the same reasons. Still, according to the United States Department of Labor, women earn an average of 24 percent less than men doing the same jobs.

Women are traditionally caregivers and often put themselves last. For example, women's careers are more interrupted by family needs. Studies demonstrate that women are primarily the family caregivers and may often be solely responsible for their children's needs as well as caring for elderly parents. Many women are having children later in life, and people are living longer. This can create dual responsibilities for women who care for parents and kids at the same time. In May of 2000, the New York Times noted one study that demonstrated that two-thirds of workers who care for elderly relatives had lost out at work by foregoing promotions, pay raises and training opportunities — and most of these workers were women.

What compounds all this is that women may also find themselves being financial caregivers as well — to both children and parents. Women are often responsible for care of an elderly parent, both financially and psychologically. Everyone needs a daughter! Women are more likely than men to serve as financial enablers — children 30 years of age or older may still be dependent on a parent for some of their income. Women, and particularly mothers, see this financial support of children as part of their role as parents. This can, however, further lead to a woman's long-term financial instability.

Sadly, divorce affects women dramatically. Fifty percent of all marriages end in divorce, and 60 percent of all subsequent marriages end in divorce. When a woman divorces, her standard of living declines as much as 45 percent in the year following a divorce. Eighty-eight percent of all divorced mothers have primary or sole custody of their children, while only 60 percent of men pay spousal support after the first two years. Actually, according to a recent state task force on gender and justice, less than 40 percent of women receive the full child support awarded. Divorce is an incredible financial drain on women.

Finally, a woman cannot assume her husband, her father or her boyfriend will take care of her. The saying goes, "A man is not a financial plan." Furthermore, a woman cannot assume her children will take care of her in her golden years, either. In fact, the states that legally require a child to support a needy parent are too few to mention. Elderly women are more often than not left to provide for themselves.

These facts place women in a unique estate planning situation in comparison to their brothers, fathers, sons and husbands. Caregivers or not, it is essential that women become aware of their special financial and estate planning needs.

Financial planning is a necessity for all generations of women to grasp and take control of their futures now, rather than be sorry they didn't later.

Women and Retirement Planning

Since women live longer, earn less and save less, this generally places them far behind men when it comes to retirement planning. Men report double the current savings amount toward retirement than women. Upon retirement, women's median pension benefit income is $3,000 — approximately two and one-half times less than a man's median pension. Ernst and Young's *Financial Planning for Women* notes that women take time off to raise families and care for elderly parents, as we have already discussed. These factors affect the amount of money earned and the amount of money saved. Married women who are nearing retirement or are currently retired are less likely than their husbands to have worked throughout their adult lives. Women take time off for childbirth, child rearing and aging parents. This has a consequence for earning potential and should be factored into an estate plan.

Married women are more likely to have changed jobs more often than men, or worked part time or seasonally as well. This is also true for single, divorced and widowed women with children. This generally means women are less prepared for retirement and their golden years when the time comes because they have had less time and means by which to contribute to retirement resources.

There are also vast differences between the sexes in investment patterns. Women are less likely to be risk takers than men, and thus are likely to be more conservative in their investing. Women take more time to investigate before they invest, but may tend to be less confident in their investing abilities than men. Some things, however, are really changing.

While historically women tend to be intimidated by financial matters, today women are starting new companies at twice the rate of men! Women now account for 12.5 percent of all Fortune 500 companies' officers, up from 11.8 percent last year and 8.75 percent in 1995. Women are getting in the game and understanding the need to be financially astute. Obviously, women possess the skills to invest wisely. Women now need confidence to take action. This book is designed to lay the foundation for giving you that confidence and to prepare you to act.

What Every Woman Wants

What does this all mean for estate planning? According to a Prudential survey, only 14 percent of women have done some form of detailed estate planning to ensure their money passes smoothly. However, 70 percent of women polled said it was important to have their money pass to their heirs. We are willing to bet that percentage is higher. We believe that *every* woman wants her assets to pass as she chooses, when she chooses and how she chooses.

Women are highly capable of making important financial decisions — they've been making the big decisions in the home for decades! Now it's time to make those decisions as part of a global strategy for your life.

But ... Do I HAVE to Do This? ... and Other Important Questions

As a woman, you need to take responsibility for yourself. Do you know what you own or how your assets are titled? Do you have a plan for your future support, possible disability and legacy? If you are widowed, this is a particularly crucial time for planning.

If you are married, do you and your husband have an estate plan? Do you know if he has a will? Do you know what your income will be if your husband were to pass away? Do you know your debts and your liabilities? Are you the beneficiary on his IRA, pension plan or life insurance policies? If your husband has to be cared for in a skilled care facility or nursing home, do you know how you will pay for his care and support yourself at home? Are you prepared to provide for your own long-term care?

If you have small children, how will you live if your husband dies? Who will care for your children if you both die, and how will that person do so? Have you provided for all your children's needs, including educational expenses, in the event of your death? Is the information organized and easy to find for those who need to know? You owe it to yourself and to your family to make sure all your financial affairs are in order.

If you are single or married, have you thought about your retirement? Fifty-three percent of women are not covered by a pension plan. You must consider now how you will provide for yourself in your retirement and your family thereafter. In her book, *Ten Smart Money Moves for Women*, Judith Briles notes that only two of every 100 seniors 65 and over are financially independent. The other 98 depend on the government, friends or relatives, or work until they die. These individuals have little or nothing to pass on to their heirs. By contrast, wouldn't you like to provide for yourself and live financially stable in your remaining years, not worrying those you love and maybe even having the opportunity to fund college for your grandchildren?

Your Legacy to Your Family

This book guides you through the simple steps it will take to save money with foresight, stay in control of your assets and leave a family legacy. It will take the intimidation out of estate planning and will allow you to plan ahead for a variety of circumstances. There are unique obstacles that women face in the path to sound estate planning. Yet this book is designed to discuss these challenges and provide solutions, guidance and insight along the way.

Women are indeed unique. There's no reason not to take control of your financial destiny for yourself and for the benefit of those you love. Every woman has a responsibility to take care of herself, and in so doing, will take care of those she loves as well. So let's get started. How you manage your estate now will be your legacy to your family.

Step 2

Find an Estate Planning Advisor

Topics Include

The Estate Planning Advisor

Working With an Estate Planning Attorney

Reasonable Fees for an Estate Planning Attorney

An Overview of the Estate Planning Process

Introduction

E STATE PLANNING: A FORMIDABLE SOUNDING ACTIVITY to many women. Confusing. Time consuming. Fraught with legal jargon and susceptible to the pitches of salespeople. Embroiled with emotion and family loyalties (and disloyalties) and reminding us of our mortality. Something perhaps better left for another day.

If you've taken the first step and opened this book, then it's clear that you are willing to spend the time necessary to create an estate plan in agreement with your personal wishes.

Or, perhaps you have a plan and realize that from time to time, it is worthwhile to review. Or, perhaps someone else has a plan for you, and you are not really sure what that is. Maybe you've relied on your husband for this area of your life. But statistics reveal that three out of every four women are single when they die.

It is important to note, and certainly motivating to hear, that despite what you might think, you do have an estate plan. Or rather, there is a plan in place. The state will select one if you don't. The question is, is it your plan or someone else's?

What Is Estate Planning?

Before answering the question "What is estate planning?" we must clarify another question: "What is your estate?" Your estate is the *total value* of all assets that you own. This includes assets held solely in your name, such as bank accounts and automobile titles, as well as assets owned jointly with others, such as your home or savings accounts. Even your life insurance, IRAs and retirement plan benefits are a part of your estate. Estate *planning*, then, is formulating specific plans to manage your assets during your lifetime in case you become incapacitated. It is also planning how to distribute your assets upon your death.

Your estate plan is your opportunity to clearly define exactly how you want the assets that will endure after you to be distributed and to whom. Also, your estate plan is a way for you to define now, while in good health, what you would like to take place with regard to your care and assets should you become incapacitated. An estate plan is a way for your preferences, experience, wisdom and dreams to benefit those people and organizations closest to your heart.

Before your plan is created, you will need to engage the services of an estate planning professional advisor.

Your Estate Planning Advisor

Most women will agree that their estate planning aspirations include providing for those they love and minimizing estate and inheritance taxes. Additionally, there are individual goals that differ from one woman to another, such as providing long-term care for an adult child with special needs, ensuring care for oneself or one's spouse should he become incapacitated, passing your business or real estate assets on to an heir or bequeathing assets to a charity.

Whatever your personal goals in regard to your estate plan, hiring qualified professionals is crucial to the success of your plan. You and your heirs will benefit from working with an estate planning team by gaining wisdom and clarity in financial decision making and keeping more money and control within your family.

Rapid changes in the area of estate planning are occurring. It is no longer sufficient to simply have an attorney prepare a WILL or invest solely in jointly held assets to avoid probate. As you will learn in this book, the challenges of estate planning are surmountable, but the process requires a professional advisor to create a plan that will meet your goals. Take a moment to look at the various professionals that might assist you. Not every woman's estate planning will require assistance from every advisor on the following page.

Whatever your goals are in regard to your estate plan, working with a qualified professional is very important. You and your heirs will benefit from working with an estate planning advisor by keeping more money and control within your family.

The Estate Planning Advisors

Financial Planner, Investment Advisor and Trust Officer

These advisors can provide needed insight regarding the correct investments, their allocation and registration. They will also assist you in considering whether a corporate trustee will be helpful for your needs.

Planned Giving Officer

These professionals also go by the title of director of planned gifts or director of development. The planned giving officer is well versed in the areas of charitable estate planning and can give you creative ideas that will maximize your charitable giving and help you achieve your estate planning goals.

Accountant

Your accountant is an essential member of the team to prepare tax returns, handle valuation issues and assist with integrating business planning and estate planning.

Life Insurance Agent

This professional will assist you with the planning and use of life insurance in estate planning. In addition, the life insurance agent is needed to keep you advised of the status of your insurance policies, recommending any changes based on your changing needs. It is critical that your life insurance policies have the correct beneficiary designations.

Estate Planning Attorney

The attorney will assist with designing the plan and will prepare the necessary legal documents and confirm that they are properly signed and work together comprehensively. Each state's laws are different. Generic forms may not work and will only leave you without a plan. Your attorney customizes your documents, being sure they allow you to take advantage of the laws of your jurisdiction, and brings your entire plan together.

What an Experienced Estate Planning Advisor Offers

Experienced estate planning advisors protect you and your ASSETS by seeing the big picture. For example, one woman astutely prepared her own will using a legal software package. Her will was technically correct. She then explained that she had just purchased a $1 million life insurance contract and wanted to name her children as the beneficiaries of the life insurance. Her will contained trusts for her children, so they would not receive their inheritance until they were 30 years old. Unfortunately, the life insurance contract listed the children as the beneficiaries rather than the trust. If the documents had been left as this conscientious mother had originally signed them, the children — if their mother had died before them — would have received their entire benefits at age 18. The life insurance proceeds would not have been controlled by her will. Although her will was correct, it did not reflect her personal wishes. This situation came to light in a meeting she had with an estate planning advisor, and a potential disaster was avoided.

When choosing an estate planning advisor, the most important consideration is that before your estate plan is designed, a face-to-face meeting takes place between you and the advisor who will help you design your plan. No two estate plans can be identical, because no two women are identical. Individual situations vary based on the amount and complexity of assets people own as well as different goals. To be successful, your estate plan must reflect your personal values, desires and aspirations. Therefore, your meeting with an estate planning advisor before your plan is designed is critical.

Estate Planning Professional Associations

Membership in one or more of the following professional associations would indicate that an attorney or other estate planning advisor is knowledgeable in estate planning. Although there are many financial organizations designed to meet the needs of women, there are no estate planning organizations designed specifically for women. There are, however, several professional associations to look for.

One such professional association is the National Association of Estate Planners and Councils. This organization offers two professional designations. One is the Accredited Estate Planner (AEP), and the other is the Estate Planning Law Specialist. To locate advisors who have received these designations, you can contact the National Association of Estate Planners and Councils at their national headquarters at 1120 Chester Avenue, Suite 470, Cleveland, OH 44114; (866) 226-2224 or e-mail at admin@naepc.org.

Another national professional association is the National Academy of Elder Law Attorneys, Inc. (NAELA). Membership in the academy is open to licensed attorneys who are practicing in the area of elder law or who are interested in legal issues pertaining to the elderly. The academy was formed in 1987 and currently has more than 3,000 members in 50 states. In 1993, NAELA formed the National Elder Law Foundation (NELF), which administers the Certified Elder Law Attorney certification. (See the appendix for more information.) For additional information, contact NAELA, 1604 N. Country Club, Tucson, AZ 85716; (520) 881-4005 or at www.naela.org.

A third professional association is the National Committee on Planned Giving. NCPG is the professional association for people whose work includes the development, marketing and administration of charitable planned gifts. This association can be contacted at NCPG, 233 McCrea Street, Suite 400, Indianapolis, IN 46225-1030; (317) 269-6274 or at www.ncpg.org.

You can determine an advisor's participation in the above associations by asking him directly, reviewing literature sent by his office or by reviewing the associations' membership lists, which can usually be found in local libraries or on the Internet.

The Estate Planning Attorney

State laws require that documents created for other people must be prepared by attorneys licensed to practice law in the state where the client resides. Therefore, virtually every estate plan will involve an attorney at some point. The following discussion is included to help you work with an estate planning attorney.

WORKING WITH AN ESTATE PLANNING ATTORNEY — WHAT TO EXPECT

Let's assume that you've obtained the name of an attorney who specializes in estate planning and is knowledgeable about tax laws. She also participates in professional associations related to estate planning. You've called the office, had a good initial conversation and set up an appointment time to explore a working relationship. At this point, the attorney's office should mail you a questionnaire prior to your office visit. This Estate Planning Questionnaire will save you time and money. Completing the form is the first important step in planning your estate.

In preparation for your initial meeting, you should bring the completed questionnaire. This will give the attorney a good understanding of you and your family situation as well as the size and complexity of your estate and an initial view of your hopes and objectives. Also, you will want to bring a copy of the DEEDS to any real estate you own and BENEFICIARY designations of your life insurance, IRAs, 401(k)s or qualified retirement plans. Being organized and prepared at that initial consultation will save you time and money later.

If you have been working with another professional advisor on your estate planning, such as an accountant, financial advisor or planned giving officer, it is appropriate to have them accompany you to your meeting with the attorney, if you so desire.

Keep in mind that the purpose of this first meeting is to describe your specific situation and determine the attorney's recommendations to help you achieve your goals. And remember, these goals include saving money on estate taxes, making sure your estate plan works for you and your life circumstances, and ensuring that the people you love receive your estate.

Another objective of the initial meeting is to determine what legal fees will be incurred if the attorney fulfills the recommendations she has made. It is also a good idea to have the attorney tell you how long it will take to complete the necessary documents. Your objective is to achieve a comprehensive and global plan for your life and estate that will benefit you and those you love.

Let's assume that this first meeting goes well and, at some point during the discussion, you decide to hire the attorney. Schedule the next meeting before leaving her office. Also, you might want to ask that the attorney have all documents prepared for you to review at your next meeting, and, if they are acceptable to you, you could then sign the documents at the second meeting. This second meeting should generally be two to three weeks after the initial meeting and should last from 45 minutes to two hours, depending on the complexity of your documents.

If you feel that you would prefer to review drafts of your documents and discuss them with other advisors before returning to the attorney's office to sign them, simply ask the attorney to send you drafts for your review and/or the review of your other professional advisors.

Of course, a first meeting might not yield enough information for the attorney to create the necessary documents, or there may be issues that need to be discussed with your spouse, children or your accountant or insurance agent. It is not unusual to need more than one visit as more time may be needed to think and review the options discussed. If this is the case, simply tell the attorney that you would like to take more time for reflection or schedule a second meeting for further review. Remember, this is a life plan, and it is important to take time and be thorough.

WHAT ARE REASONABLE FEES FOR AN ESTATE PLANNING ATTORNEY?

You've located an experienced attorney, talked on the phone, met in her office and are ready to move forward. What would be considered reasonable fees for her services? How much should you expect to pay for your estate planning documents?

Billing Arrangements

Fixed Fee (also known as Established Fee)

Under the fixed fee approach, an attorney will quote you a fixed fee to do the work she is engaged to do. Often attorneys offer you a package rate that covers all the services you will need to set up your estate plan.

Quoting an Estimated Range of Fees

It is difficult for attorneys to charge a fixed fee for complex services. This is because every case is different and the attorney is never completely sure of the amount of time and energy a client will require. For this reason, many attorneys quote an estimated range of fees.

Hourly Billing

Some attorneys will simply charge by the hour at an agreed-upon rate for the time spent working on your estate plan. Based on experience or professional affiliation, a regional average for an attorney in rural Virginia might be in the range of $125 – $175 per hour while in Long Island, N.Y., the average might change to $200 – $300.

This question is like asking how much a car should cost. Is it a new car? Is it a used car? Is it a Cooper Mini? Is it a

Cadillac? There are so many variables that it is not possible to specify what a reasonable fee for legal services rendered should be. You will need to do some research pertinent to your individual situation. The best approach is to ask two or three attorneys to give you an estimate of their fees. Then you will have an idea of the range of legal fees related to the preparation of the estate plan. Always keep in mind that the lowest fee should not be the only criteria for choosing an estate planning attorney.

Most attorneys base their fees on one of the three billing arrangements noted on the previous page. The billing arrangement should be clearly communicated to you prior to the onset of your legal work.

An Overview of the Estate Planning Process

The process of planning your estate involves many considerations, discussions and assessments of what is important to you, your heirs and your favorite charities. For some women, this process will entail nothing more than determining whom they would name as guardians of their minor children. For others with more complex estates, there will be many more considerations.

It is helpful to separate the estate planning process into six phases. The time necessary to proceed through all six of these phases can be as short as two or three weeks or as long as two or three years, depending upon your specific situation. The following explanation of the estate planning process is not a rigid outline but is intended to provide an overview. Let's start with Phase One ...

Phase One: Gather the Necessary Information

Gathering your documents together for your team to review is the first step in creating your comprehensive plan.

Completing the Estate Planning Questionnaire mentioned earlier in this chapter is also part of the first step. You will use the questionnaire to define and specify the rest of the information you will need.

Family Information

These are the people who will be affected by your planning. This includes family members as well as other people who you desire to receive (or not receive!) a portion of your estate. Be sure to include their names and addresses.

Financial Information

Accurate financial information is critical to your estate plan. It is important to have an inventory listing your assets and LIABILITIES. In addition to listing the current value of your assets, it is also important to confirm how they are TITLED. Other information needed includes life insurance policies and retirement plan benefits.

Establish Your Goals and Put Them in Writing

Your estate plan is as individual as you are. Nevertheless, typical goals might be:

- Plan to make your assets last throughout your lifetime.

- Confirm that your assets reach the people and charities you choose while avoiding family conflict over your estate.

- Minimize your estate's losses to taxes, excess legal fees and expenses and avoid forced sale of assets to pay these costs.

- Prevent heirs from squandering their inheritance.

Name Those Who Will Carry Out Your Wishes

You will need to consider who you wish to serve as the executor to settle your estate. In addition, if you are preparing any trusts in your plan, you will want to begin thinking about who you would appoint to serve as TRUSTEE. If you have minor children, you should name a GUARDIAN to care for them. Lastly, regarding possible incapacity, it would be important to consider who should serve as the agent in your POWER OF ATTORNEY and your LIVING WILL.

PHASE TWO: ESTIMATE TAXES AND EXPENSES DUE UNDER YOUR EXISTING ESTATE PLAN

As mentioned earlier, whether you've created one or not, an estate plan is in place with regard to your assets. Unfortunately, your state's plan or the court's plan may not be identical to your wishes. Before implementing your plan, it is helpful to calculate the taxes and expenses that would be payable from your estate at death under your existing plan. It is also important to determine the LIQUID ASSETS available to pay these last expenses and taxes.

PHASE THREE: DESIGN A NEW ESTATE PLAN

The third step in the process is to design an estate plan to accomplish your unique goals and objectives at the least cost. This requires thought and planning on your part, using the assistance of your estate planning advisor.

PHASE FOUR: IMPLEMENT THE PLAN

After you and your estate planning team have reviewed and agreed upon your estate plan, the plan should be implemented. This includes your attorney's preparation and drafting of the documents necessary. Additional steps would be acquiring life insurance or long-term care insurance, if necessary, reregistering assets and changing the beneficiary designation on IRAs, qualified retirement plans and life insurance. Gifts to charity should be thoroughly discussed as they offer many benefits to a good estate plan. All of this activity would occur using the services of the members of your estate planning team.

PHASE FIVE: MAKE A SECOND CALCULATION OF TAXES AND EXPENSES

After the plan has been designed and implemented, it is important to make a second calculation of taxes and expenses payable from your estate at death. The savings in taxes and expenses will give you a sense of accomplishment and peace of mind that the plan has been implemented to reflect your concerns and protect your estate.

PHASE SIX: MONITOR YOUR ESTATE PLAN

In addition to changes in taxes and laws, women's lives and families are in a constant state of flux with regard to relationships, marriages, deaths, births or adoptions and personal income or the value of assets. For this reason, it is important to monitor your estate plan. The plan should be reviewed every two to three years in light of the changes in your life as well as the changes in laws and taxation. You may want to get in the habit of checking to see if your plan needs to be updated each fall when planning personal and professional goals for the coming year.

Summary

Like many worthwhile activities, estate planning is a process and not an event. The process begins by retaining an attorney with experience in trusts and tax laws. Your preparation in defining estate planning goals and assembling other important advisors, such as an accountant and life insurance agent, will ensure a smooth process. Never underestimate the importance of face-to-face meetings with your advisor and establish a set time every two or three years to monitor your plan and keep it up to date.

Step 3

Understand the Estate Planning Fundamentals

Introduction

*I*T IS HUMAN NATURE to avoid tasks that are confusing and seem complex, especially where money and family are involved. Plus, there are a lot of things we would rather do — clean out closets, weed the garden and repaint the living room (!) — than give serious thought to what will happen to our estate after we die. Neither are we eager to envision ourselves mentally or physically incapacitated. Still, reality exists, time marches on and we must do our best with that over which we can exercise some control. Planning our estate is one aspect where a woman can demonstrate consideration and financial wisdom for the people and organizations she cares about the most.

Some of the confusion and mystery that surrounds the world of estate planning can be attributed to trying to handle the plan in a piecemeal manner. A piecemeal approach is like having someone explain the particular moves of the chess pieces without ever explaining the various strategies of chess. The purpose of this chapter is to lay the groundwork regarding the fundamentals of estate planning and approach the estate planning process with an understanding of how various parts of the plan relate to one another. In this way, we can develop an overall strategy that meets your goals.

We will discuss how assets pass at death, the probate process, DISCLAIMERS and spousal elections. It is important to gain a clear understanding of the fundamentals so that you can incorporate the material in later chapters within the broader picture of your personal estate plan.

What Happens to Your Assets at Death Depends Upon "How" You Own Them

ASSETS IN YOUR NAME ONLY (PROBATE ASSETS)

Upon death, assets you own in your name alone are called PROBATE ASSETS. In a strict sense, probate refers to the legal process that affects such assets. Probate, as understood by most people, however, refers to the estate settlement process. This includes probating the will as well as paying taxes and filing papers with the court.

Estate settlement, with regard to probate assets, is the process of changing the title of assets from the name of a deceased person into the name of her appropriate heir. It requires notifying both family members and the public that one has died, confirming that the rightful owners receive their inheritance and giving creditors of the decedent an opportunity to present their bills for payment. The decedent's executor undertakes this process, and there are fees incurred by the estate to complete it. Attorney's fees and executor's commissions, with respect to settling an estate, are not specified by law in many states, but it is not unusual for both the attorney and the executor to be compensated 5% of the gross estate value. Many attorneys follow a fee schedule based on a percentage of the value of the estate. Other attorneys bill for their services on an hourly basis.

The time required to settle an estate is based on a number of factors including the size of the estate, the complexity of the assets and family harmony, or lack of it. An average time frame to settle a medium-sized estate would be six to 12 months. If you die with a will, you are known as a TESTATRIX. When someone dies without a will, she is said to have died INTESTATE.

Probate Assets

A person's probate estate is made up of only those assets that must go through the probate process before they can be distributed to the heirs. Probate assets include property that is:

- owned solely by the decedent;

- owned jointly with others as tenants in common; and

- life insurance, annuities, IRAs and other assets that have no named beneficiary or that name the decedent's estate.

Who Gets What When Someone Dies Without a Will

Every state has unique laws governing who receives the estate of someone who dies without a will. Your attorney will advise you as to the laws in your state regarding asset distribution upon death. Just as an example, Pennsylvania's laws of intestacy are listed below:

Married Individuals

If you have a husband or wife who survives you and you have no children and your parents are not living, then your spouse would inherit your entire estate. If you have no children, but one or more parents, then your spouse gets the first $30,000 and half of the balance. Your surviving parents get the remaining half.

Married With Children

If you and your surviving spouse have children, your spouse gets the first $30,000 and half of the balance. The children get equal shares of the remaining half.

If you and your spouse have children and you also have children who are not from your marriage with your spouse, your spouse gets half of your estate and all of your children get equal shares of the other half.

Estates of Single Individuals

If you have any children, each would get equal shares of your estate. Otherwise, your estate would go to the persons who are living at your death in this order of priority:

- your parents;
- your brothers and sisters, or their children;
- your grandparents;
- your uncles and aunts or their descendants; and
- the Commonwealth of Pennsylvania.

ASSETS OWNED JOINTLY WITH OTHERS (NONPROBATE ASSETS)

What about assets that you own with others; are they controlled by your will? The distribution of assets that you own jointly with others is not controlled by your will. These assets will be controlled BY OPERATION OF LAW. This means that upon your death, your jointly owned assets will *automatically and instantly* belong to those who jointly own them. It cannot be emphasized enough that whether assets are owned jointly between spouses or nonspouses, the distribution of such assets upon death *will not be controlled by your will*. This is important to remember since the work done in your will or living trust would be worthless if all of your assets are owned jointly.

There are three ways two or more people can own the same asset at the same time: JOINT TENANTS WITH RIGHTS OF SURVIVORSHIP, TENANTS BY THE ENTIRETY and TENANTS IN COMMON.

Nonprobate Assets

Nonprobate assets are identified by how they are titled and consist of all assets that are not probate assets, such as:

- assets held jointly with others as joint tenants with rights of survivorship or tenants by the entirety;

- assets payable to a named beneficiary (life insurance, annuity and IRAs, for example); and

- assets promised to others by written agreement (partnership agreement, separation agreement or shareholder's agreement, for example).

Joint Tenants With Rights of Survivorship

This form of joint ownership specifies that when one asset owner dies, the surviving owners automatically receive the deceased owner's share. This type of joint property is not controlled by the owner's will. Assets owned in this manner are typically owned by nonspouses. One disadvantage is that this joint tenancy can be broken by only one joint owner who can sell his interest.

Tenants by the Entirety

In many states, assets held jointly by a husband and wife are known as tenants by the entirety. This means that each has an undivided interest in the whole and that neither the husband nor the wife alone can sell or transfer the asset. It can only be transferred by *both* spouses and is not controlled by either of their wills.

Tenants in Common

Assets held in this form of joint ownership are controlled by your will. This form of ownership means that when one owner dies, her share of the joint asset will remain a part of her estate and go to her heirs under her will.

Mother and Daughter Tale of Joint Ownership

Mother Martin is 80 years old and has lived in the family home for 60 years. Her husband passed away many years ago. The Martins had one daughter, Elizabeth. Mother wants Elizabeth to inherit the family home when she dies. To smooth this transition, Mother made Elizabeth a joint owner in the home by putting Elizabeth's name on the deed. At Mother's death, the house will pass to Elizabeth free of the probate process. The creation of the joint ownership, however, was a taxable gift from Mrs. Martin to her daughter. No tax may be due, but if the value of the gift exceeds $11,000, a federal gift tax return will be required.

Although they do avoid probate, one disadvantage with jointly owned assets is the fact that the creditors of any one of the joint owners can attack the asset to the extent of the owner's interest therein. (This is not true for tenants by the entirety assets.)

Accidental Disinheritance Woes

Mr. and Mrs. Smith are married, and Mrs. Smith dies. Mr. Smith, who manages a large farm that has been in his family for many years, eventually remarries and retitles the farm into joint names with himself and his second wife. Smith's will has been in place for some time, specifying that upon his death, all of his assets will pass on to his children from his first marriage. He has a life insurance policy designating the new Mrs. Smith as beneficiary, so he feels she will be taken care of and the farm can stay in the family. Unbeknownst to Smith, however, is that even if his will gives everything to his children upon his death, the farm would automatically be owned by his current wife because the farm deed lists Mr. Smith and this second wife as joint owners.

ASSETS GIVEN TO OTHERS BY BENEFICIARY DESIGNATION OR AGREEMENTS (NONPROBATE ASSETS)

Nonprobate assets are not controlled by your will. Annuities, retirement plans, IRAs, separation agreements with estate provisions, SHAREHOLDER AGREEMENTS and partnership agreements are all examples of nonprobate assets. Life insurance policies are also nonprobate assets. Nonprobate assets are distributed to the designated beneficiary regardless of what the will states.

When you purchase a life insurance policy, you are asked to name a beneficiary to receive the benefits of the policy upon your death. Regardless of what your will says, the proceeds will be paid directly to the beneficiaries you named in the life insurance contract. This is why it is important to coordinate your will with your life insurance.

The precise wording of beneficiary designation forms is important. Preprinted forms may not permit the listing of your wishes, so always confirm with your insurance agent exactly what you want to have happen with regard to life insurance benefits. Life and the circumstances of your family may change over time, and you should periodically review beneficiary forms to confirm their continued accuracy.

Who, What and When

Helen knows that if she dies unexpectedly, her estate will leave a substantial inheritance to her minor children, who are now teenagers. Therefore, her will states that the children are not to receive their inheritance until they reach age 25. It will also be essential that Helen not designate as her life insurance beneficiary "my children." She will need to designate the trust in her will as the beneficiary of the life insurance, because the life insurance is not controlled by the will, and if the beneficiary simply said "my children," they would receive their entire inheritance at age 18. Helen would rather see her children spend their inheritance on graduate school at age 25 than on a Corvette at age 18.

Why Comprehensive Estate Planning Is Important

Now that you know there are three different forms of ownership that control how your assets are distributed at death, you understand why it is important to review your beneficiary designations and security registrations as well as deeds and other accounts to confirm how each is titled.

When to Review Your Estate Plan, Including Wills, Deeds, Insurance Policies and Annuities

- Marriage (your own or another family member's)
- Retirement planning
- Divorce
- Moving to another state
- The birth of a child
- An adoption
- Disability or prolonged illness in the family
- Children reaching adulthood
- Selling real estate
- Purchasing real estate
- Purchasing life insurance
- Starting or disbanding a business
- An inheritance from a parent or grandparent
- A death in the family
- A significant increase or reduction in assets

As you complete your will, do not forget to review all of the following that apply to you:

YOU HAVE NO WILL

This means that your estate plan has been established by your state legislators. They have set out rules for the distribution of your estate when you die without a will, whether you know what those rules are or not. Furthermore, a court will decide who will care for your children, whether you think that person is going to be the best parent for your child or not.

THE DEED TO YOUR HOME OR OTHER PROPERTY

If you own property with another person, when the title agent or attorney prepared the deed for your home, she probably designated the deed as joint tenants with rights of survivorship (or perhaps tenants by the entirety if you are married).

LIFE INSURANCE

When you purchased your life insurance, the agent asked you to name the beneficiary of the policy. That beneficiary designation is a part of your estate plan.

IRAs

When you invested in your IRA at the bank or in a mutual fund, you named a beneficiary. Determining who the recipient of that IRA will be at your death is part of your estate plan.

ANNUITIES

Annuity contracts name a designated beneficiary to receive the annuity funds at the death of the owner. The investment advisor asked you, at some point, who should be named as the beneficiary of your annuities.

TRANSFER ON DEATH OR PAYABLE ON DEATH ACCOUNTS

Any bank accounts with payable on death designations or securities that you registered with your investment advisor as a T.O.D. account is a part of your estate plan.

YOUR WILL

Lastly, there is your will, the one plan that receives the most thoughtful consideration. The person who prepares your will also needs to help you confirm how your name is listed on your deed or who the beneficiaries are of your life insurance, IRAs, annuities and transfer on death accounts. As you can see, it is critical to approach estate planning from a *comprehensive* perspective, one that considers all angles and involves all the assets that you own.

Postmortem Estate Planning

One important aspect of estate planning is called postmortem estate planning. This refers to strategies to complete or make corrections to an estate plan after one's death. There are a number of tax elections that can be done postmortem as well as the right of the surviving spouse to elect against the estate (see page 35). Another area of postmortem estate planning relates to the use of DISCLAIMERS. The following sections describe spousal election rights and disclaimers as used in postmortem estate planning.

Surviving Spouse's Right to Elect Against the Estate

In many states, whether a will exists or not, and no matter what a will or living trust specifies, a surviving spouse has a *legal right* to inherit up to one-half of the estate of the deceased spouse when the first spouse dies. This is known as the spousal elective share or the ELECTIVE SHARE rule. (The estate of the deceased spouse is adjusted for certain distributions made during his lifetime.) The purpose of the elective share rule is to prevent one spouse from disinheriting the other by confirming that the surviving spouse will at least have a *minimal* share of the decedent's estate.

The assets over which the surviving spouse has the right to make the election include those that pass from the deceased spouse by will or intestacy. Assets conveyed by the decedent during marriage to himself and another with rights of survivorship are also included in his estate. Typically, transfers in which the decedent retained some interest in the property, life insurance and employee benefits are also included in his estate. Lastly, assets that were given away by the decedent within one year of death to the extent that the gift exceeded $3,000 to each donee are subject to this election in some states.

This is a legal right that can be lost if one spouse forfeits her right by deserting the deceased spouse during her lifetime. Also, the use of a PREMARITAL AGREEMENT may eliminate the possibility of a spouse electing against the estate.

> The elective share rule is an election that the surviving spouse must affirmatively make in order to receive the elective share. Although state laws differ, the request for election must be filed no later than six months after qualification of the will for probate, or qualification of the intestate administrator if there is no will.

DISCLAIMERS

To disclaim means to give up all rights that you have in something that legally would belong to you if you did not disclaim your interest in it. For example, you can disclaim an interest in an asset that you are entitled to receive as an inheritance under a will. You can also disclaim life insurance cash proceeds you are entitled to under the beneficiary designation of life insurance or an IRA. You can even disclaim an interest that you would receive by being a joint owner of an asset if one of the other joint owners should die. State laws allow a person to disclaim any interest in any asset that she is entitled to receive and thereby give up any rights in that interest. The interest disclaimed can be either the entire interest or a portion of the interest.

The requirements for a valid disclaimer are: (1) it must describe the property interest disclaimed, (2) it must declare the disclaimer and the extent thereof and (3) it must be signed by the disclaimant, dated and notarized.

The disclaimer is irrevocable, and the asset cannot be retrieved once it has been disclaimed. In the event of a disclaimer, the law treats the disclaimant as having predeceased the decedent, and the interest will pass as though the disclaimant had died before the transfer was made. For this reason, one should be diligent in confirming exactly to whom the disclaimed interest will go once the disclaimer is filed.

WHAT ARE THE BENEFITS OF DISCLAIMING?

As a part of postmortem estate planning, disclaiming is a strategy often used to do federal estate tax planning after death. For example, if the wife had CREDIT SHELTER TRUST provisions in her will but owned all of her assets jointly with her husband, the only way that assets could be used to fund the wife's credit shelter trust after her death would be for her husband to disclaim his wife's one-half interest in the joint assets that he would inherit by operation of law. As a result of his disclaimer, the wife's one-half interest does not go to the husband by operation of law; instead, the wife's interest is now controlled by her will and will be available to fund her credit shelter trust. This will allow her property to pass to her children free of federal estate taxes.

IRS Requirements for a Valid Disclaimer

Disclaiming is often done for federal tax purposes. The disclaimer must qualify under the Internal Revenue Code §2518 as well as state law when disclaiming for federal tax purposes. The requirements under Internal Revenue Code §2518 for a qualified disclaimer are as follows:

- The disclaimer must be an irrevocable refusal to accept an interest;

- The disclaimer must be in writing, dated and notarized;

- The disclaimer must be delivered to the person making the transfer or the holder of the legal title to the assets to which the interest relates no later than nine months after the date of the transfer creating the interest or the date disclaimant becomes 21;

- The disclaimant must not have accepted the disclaimed interest or any of its benefits;

- The disclaimed interest must pass without any direction on the part of the disclaimant; and

- The disclaimer must be without qualification.

One key provision regarding disclaimers is that they must be filed before accepting any interest in the assets being disclaimed. Once one has accepted the benefit of any assets, he or she will be barred from disclaiming any interest in the assets accepted.

Another use of disclaimers is with annuities. For example, Mrs. Smith owns a $100,000 annuity that is payable to the children of her first marriage at her death. Upon her death, it is determined that there would be state inheritance tax and federal estate tax due upon the amounts inherited by her children. If, in this case, the children were to disclaim their interests in the annuity, the annuity would be payable to Mrs. Smith's estate. Estate assets are controlled by her will, and Mrs. Smith's will directs that her assets be given to her husband to qualify for the marital deduction. The result of her children's disclaimer is that no tax is due on the annuities. There are many other instances where the use of a disclaimer will permit assets to pass to others at lower tax rates.

HOW ARE DISCLAIMERS INVOKED?

Once it is determined that the estate plan of a deceased person would be improved if one of the beneficiaries disclaimed his interest, notice of his intent to disclaim must be provided to the one transferring the interest no later than *nine months after the date of death*. That notice must be given directly to the one making the transfer. A copy of the notice can be filed at the city or county's probate court and date-stamped to confirm the timing of the disclaimer.

DISCLAIMER OF JOINTLY OWNED ASSETS

The IRS permits jointly owned assets to be disclaimed whether the jointly owned assets are held as joint tenants with rights of survivorship or held by husband and wife as tenants by the entirety. In either case, the surviving joint tenant is permitted to file a disclaimer within *nine months* of the date of death of the first joint tenant to die, disclaiming the asset interest he is entitled to receive by operation of law.

Rules Regarding Disclaimers of Jointly Owned Assets by a Surviving Spouse

All jointly owned assets can be placed in one of two categories.

Category #1

Depending on who contributed the funds into the account, it may be possible for a surviving spouse to disclaim the entire balance in such an account within nine months of the first spouse's death. This includes joint accounts created in banks, brokerage firms and other investment accounts such as mutual funds.

Category #2

The second category includes joint tenancies created in all other types of assets. If the assets in this category were owned solely by the two spouses, it is only possible for a surviving spouse to disclaim a maximum of one-half of the interest in their joint assets when the first spouse dies.

Summary

Before you can define what estate planning is, you must recognize the many assets that make up your estate. Once those assets are listed, you can identify if they are probate or nonprobate assets and then determine if you have the proper beneficiaries designated and a clear understanding of what is and is not governed by your will. As life situations change and as you may have had the input of several different professionals at different times, it's important to ensure that your plan is up-to-date, comprehensive and consistent with your goals.

Where joint ownership is concerned, you can confirm that your wishes are carried out by having a clear understanding of the three types of joint ownership. Also, it is imperative that you understand the benefits of both the elective share rule and postmortem estate planning, such as disclaimers.

Step 4

Stay in Control of Your Assets as You Move Through the Seasons of Life

Topics Include

Management by Power of Attorney

Healthcare Power of Attorney

The Living Will

Planning for Nursing Home Costs

Long-Term Care Insurance

Trusts for Family Members with Disabilities

Introduction

*E*VERY WOMAN, especially as she approaches midlife (or when she suddenly realizes that she qualifies for a senior citizen discount), wonders what will happen to her if she become incapacitated, either short term or long term. A heart attack, a stroke, a battle with cancer or simply slipping on an icy sidewalk can change your life in ways we really don't like to think about: Who will help with preparing meals or driving me to doctor appointments? Will I have to move in with my children? What if I have no children or what if they live far away and cannot help? What if I'm already caring for an ill spouse or elderly parent … *I can't afford to get sick!*

While the natural tendency is to avoid topics that make us uncomfortable, doing whatever possible now, while in good health, to prepare for the future is reassuring. This chapter describes planning strategies to address the concerns that arise in the event you do become incapacitated. This chapter also covers helpful plans in case of the INCAPACITY of a family member, whether a child (adult or minor) that is disabled or one of your parents who is in a nursing home or has other needs.

Planning for possible incapacity involves maintaining the financial well-being of the incapacitated person as well as planning for his or her personal care. Failure to make any plans to deal with incapacity could result in a court-appointed GUARDIAN managing your affairs. Few women would want a complete stranger to handle their affairs. Guardianship can be avoided through careful planning.

Who Will Manage Your Assets if You Become Incapacitated?

State laws typically define an incapacitated person as an adult whose ability to receive and evaluate information and communicate decisions is impaired to such a significant extent that she is unable to manage her financial resources or to meet essential requirements for her physical health and safety. The mere presence of poor judgment, mental illness or a physical disability does not render one an incapacitated person. People who are disabled do not lose their rights to self-determination simply because they are disabled. Women may be particularly concerned about this as they tend to be caregivers rather than care receivers. Knowing how things work, and planning beforehand, however, can alleviate all your concerns.

MANAGEMENT BY YOUR COURT-APPOINTED GUARDIAN

If you became incapacitated and did not make any plans beforehand, you would require a court-appointed guardian to take care of you. If a court determines you are incapacitated and in need of assistance regarding only your financial affairs, a conservator (in some states known as "a guardian of the estate") will be appointed to manage your bank accounts, bills and any other areas specified by the court order. If you would be unable to make decisions regarding your personal care, a guardian (in some states known as "a guardian of the person") will be appointed to make decisions such as where you will live and how you will be cared for. If both a guardian and conservator are appointed, they may be the same person, or the court may appoint a different person for each role. Generally, a guardian "over the person" must sign a bond promising a faithful execution of her duties. Depending on the size and amount of an incapacitated person's financial affairs, a conservator "of the estate" is also generally required to execute a bond. In addition, the court will specify any limitations placed on the incapacitated person, such as whether the person is able to retain the right to vote.

The expense, publicity and delay caused by the guardianship hearings, court deliberations and issuance of a court order can all be avoided by proper planning.

POWER OF ATTORNEY AND MANAGEMENT BY YOUR NAMED AGENT

As mentioned earlier, few women would choose to have a stranger make all their financial and healthcare decisions for them. This is all the more reason why it is so important to have plans in place in the event you become incapacitated. Let's look at the documents that should be prepared now, before illness or injury strike.

A POWER OF ATTORNEY is a document that gives another person or institution named by you the right to take certain actions on your behalf. The scope of actions authorized is written within the power of attorney. You are the PRINCIPAL who signs the power of attorney, and the person given the authority to act on your behalf is called the AGENT (in some states known as the "attorney-in-fact"). A valid power of attorney that names an appropriate agent avoids the guardianship procedure, provided there are no guardianship services needed that are not specified in the power of attorney.

Plenary Guardianship
(guardian and conservator)

Total responsibility for the incapacitated person. Responsibility over healthcare, finances, assets, living arrangements, property ... total responsibility.

Limited Guardianships
(may be either the guardian or the conservator)

Responsibility is specified by court decree. For example: managing finances, making healthcare decisions, handling living arrangements, etc.

How Guardianship and Conservatorship Are Established by the Court

1. Petition is filed with the court.
2. Notice is given to the alleged incapacitated person and her next of kin.
3. In many states, the court appoints a guardian ad litem to represent the interests of the alleged incapacitated person. The guardian ad litem investigates the situation and reports to the court about the capacity or lack thereof of the individual in question.
4. A time and place (in the city or county where the person lives) of a court hearing to determine incapacity is set.
5. Evidence is presented regarding the person's incapacity.
6. The court determines whether there is a need for guardianship or conservatorship.
7. The court appoints an individual, a corporate fiduciary or an agency as guardian or conservator.
8. The guardian or conservator is required to file an annual report and accounting with the court.

TYPES OF POWERS OF ATTORNEY

A GENERAL POWER OF ATTORNEY gives the agent broad power to do almost anything for the principal. The general power of attorney is valid upon delivery to the agent and is commonly used for the convenience of the principal or to plan for possible future disability.

A LIMITED POWER OF ATTORNEY gives the agent the power to do only specific things spelled out in the document.

Generally, a power of attorney is effective as soon as it is signed unless it contains language stating that it will not go into effect until the principal is unable to handle her own affairs. This language creates a SPRINGING POWER OF ATTORNEY. One difficulty with the springing power of attorney is that the agent must have proof that the principal is incapacitated in order to gain the legal authority to serve as an agent. The proof can generally be provided by a certification of incapacity by a physician, but some banks or investment firms might prefer a court order of incapacity. This defeats the purpose for having a power of attorney. Nonetheless, even though court proceedings may be necessary, at least the person named could take control rather than a stranger appointed by the court.

A DURABLE POWER OF ATTORNEY will remain in effect if the principal later becomes mentally incapacitated. Many states' laws require language indicating that the principal intends for the power of attorney to remain in effect even upon and throughout the principal's disability. Almost all powers of attorney executed by lawyers contain these durable provisions. Since there is no reason not to use the word "durable," it is preferred that the word be used when your intent is that the agent will continue to have legal authority as agent if you become incapacitated.

Preparing a Power of Attorney

A power of attorney requires the principal's signature. To protect you and your assets, banks and other financial institutions often require the power of attorney to be prepared by a lawyer. This lawyer should be knowledgeable about what language should be in the document in order to accomplish the principal's goals and give the agent the needed authority to do so.

After the Power of Attorney Is Signed

- You, as the principal, can revoke the power of attorney at any time, as long as you are competent. If you are no longer competent, a guardian can be appointed and the power of attorney revoked in that proceeding. If you choose to revoke your power of attorney, you should notify the agent and all relevant institutions.

- Be sure that your agent is willing to use the power of attorney when necessary. Instruct your agent not to use the power of attorney while you are competent, unless you ask her to do so.

- Make sure your agent knows where your power of attorney is kept, so that she will have access to it if you become incapacitated. If you keep it in your safety deposit box, make sure your agent can get into that box when need be.

- You may want to let your agent keep the power of attorney in her possession.

- The agent should always keep at least one original copy of the power of attorney when she is using it.

- Tell your agent that she must sign as follows when she signs for you when using your power of attorney: (your name) by (agent's name), agent for (your name). Then it will be clear that she is signing on your behalf only.

With regard to the power of attorney, it is important to understand that the death of the principal ends the authority of the agent. In other words, when you die, your agent no longer has any authority to act on your behalf. Sometimes children who have served as agent under a power of attorney for an elderly parent attempt to withdraw money from the bank to pay funeral expenses after their parent has died. They are surprised to discover that the bank no longer honors the power of attorney because the parent is deceased. Only the executor named in the will can gain access to the money after the death of a parent.

Husbands and wives usually appoint each other as their agents and name adult children as successor agents. If husband and wife each name the other as the initial agent, there is little danger in having an immediate power of attorney. Indeed, having an immediate power of attorney would be a help if one spouse is unavailable to sign any documents that would require both signatures, such as a deed for the sale of real estate.

Essential Benefits of the Power of Attorney

1. It provides a means to manage the finances of the incapacitated person. There is no need to tie up investments during the course of a guardianship procedure.

2. It can give permission to the agent to make gifts on behalf of the principal. In order for an incapacitated person's agent to make gifts, he or she must have that authority specified in the power of attorney.

3. If husband and wife owned real estate jointly, in order to sell the real estate, both signatures would be required. If one spouse is incapacitated, a guardianship hearing could be avoided with a power of attorney.

There is no restriction as to the number of people that can be named as agent in a power of attorney. The law provides a list of specified powers that may be incorporated into your power of attorney. These powers are not required to be listed in full, but can be referred to in summary form. Listing in full, however, will confirm to others your intent. You may also grant powers to your agents that are in addition to those listed in the law.

MANAGEMENT BY THE SUCCESSOR TRUSTEE NAMED IN YOUR LIVING TRUST

LIVING TRUSTS are another strategy to plan for incapacity. In a living trust, you can appoint a primary trustee and a successor trustee (who would control the assets should the primary trustee become incapacitated). Please see the next chapter for a detailed discussion on living trusts.

Mr. and Mrs. Miller and Their Not-So-Secret Agents

Mr. and Mrs. Miller have three children. They can appoint each other as primary agent and their three children as alternate agents with the provision that any one of the three children can act alone as agent under the power of attorney. An alternative is to require the signatures of all three children to take any action using the power of attorney, or, that child A would serve, but if unavailable, then child B would serve as alternate and child C as successor alternate.

Who Will Make Your Healthcare Decisions if You Become Incapacitated?

THE ADVANCE MEDICAL DIRECTIVE

Residents of many states commonly use an advance medical directive to allow a person to declare her desires for healthcare should she become incapacitated and unable to do so.

This document typically has two parts. The first part is a declaration of your end-of-life wishes. This is also known as a living will. The second part of the document names someone to make medical decisions for you if you are unable to make them yourself. This is known as a healthcare power of attorney. We will discuss each of these documents separately below.

HEALTHCARE POWER OF ATTORNEY

A HEALTHCARE POWER OF ATTORNEY is a power of attorney used to appoint a healthcare agent to make healthcare decisions for the principal including decisions relating to life-sustaining treatment. The language in your healthcare power of attorney should be very specific regarding your intent (not your lawyer's intent, not your husband's intent, not your daughter's or son's intent) so your agent knows exactly what you want. The directive is usually not legally binding unless the principal is unable to make his or her wishes known. These documents are different for each state jurisdiction.

In April of 2003, a new law took effect that has created many headaches for those using healthcare powers of attorneys. The law is known as "The Health Insurance Portability and Accountability Act" or HIPAA. The purpose of HIPAA is to protect medical privacy. Under HIPAA, medical providers must take great care not to disseminate "Protected Health Information" which is defined as just about everything about a patient. The penalties to the medical provider for noncompliance with the HIPAA privacy rules can run from $100 per violation to criminal penalties of up to $50,000 in fines and a year in prison.

HIPAA does permit disclosure of information to a "personal representative." A personal representative is someone who has the legal authority to make medical decisions for the patient. While an agent under a valid power of attorney or a surrogate appointed under a valid advance medical directive or healthcare power of attorney is a personal representative, the problem is that medical providers are so afraid of breaking the law and incurring penalties that they are very cautious and may not know whether or not the general power of attorney or medical directive is sufficient authority for them to release the information.

Therefore, many medical providers look for a specific reference to HIPAA and if they see none, they may be afraid that the document does not permit them to release the medical information. Therefore, your healthcare power of attorney should contain language with specific references to HIPAA. Be sure to have your attorney point out to you in your healthcare power of attorney the language she includes to deal with the HIPAA challenges.

Living Will

Advances in the field of medical care and lifestyle differences make it possible for many people to live fully and vibrantly well into their 80s. We all have definite beliefs and desires concerning our wishes should we become incapacitated and dependent on medical technology to keep us alive. Without a living will, someone you may not have chosen will be responsible for making decisions regarding your end-of-life care.

A living will is a document that gives directions to your treating physicians concerning your end-of-life care in the event that you are unable to communicate due to being incapacitated and either terminally ill or in a coma.

Living wills state that "life-prolonging procedures" are to be withheld or withdrawn if you are terminally ill or in a coma. A life-prolonging procedure is any medical procedure serving only to delay the natural dying process. This includes artificial feeding (called nutrition and hydration), CPR, kidney dialysis and antibiotics, for example. The living will does not prevent the use of medication or medical procedures to reduce pain.

One thing that absolutely separates women from men is the ability to be pregnant. For this reason, women need to be all the more thoughtful about medical directives that may take effect to the harm of their unborn babies. Every woman who has ever been a mother understands the extremely altruistic nature of motherhood. Most mothers are willing to give their lives for their children. If you are of childbearing years, consider placing a provision in your living will, advance medical directive or healthcare proxy that protects the life of your unborn child, even in the event of your incapacity. Perhaps you would like to mention in your documents an exception to life support if you are pregnant so that the life of your unborn child would be protected.

If you prefer variations of these procedures, have your attorney customize your living will rather than using a pre-printed form. Your attorney can integrate all of your desires for life-sustaining procedures.

Who Will Pay for Your Care if You Cannot Take Care of Yourself?

PAYING FOR LONG-TERM CARE AT HOME OR IN A LONG-TERM CARE FACILITY

Life expectancy has increased with each generation and is on the average seven years longer for women than for men. Yet healthcare costs have continued to increase. A growing concern of many women is the depletion of their assets to pay for nursing home care. There is good cause for concern. Women make up 85% of nursing home occupants! And the average monthly cost of nursing home care in Pennsylvania, for example, is $5,560; it is $8,695 in New York; and in Virginia, it is $4,502. Just using these three averages, the average annual cost of long-term care is $75,000+. A three-year stay in a nursing home approaches a quarter of a million dollars. Two questions immediately arise: "Who will pay for these services?" and "Will I outlive my money by paying for these services?"

Many people assume that the government will pay for their nursing home care, but there is no government program to pay the nursing home or long-term care expenses of those who can afford to pay for these services themselves.

The government has established two insurance programs that *may* pay for some of these healthcare services: Medicare and MEDICAID. Medicare is a government health insurance program with an automatic enrollment for all persons, regardless of income, who are age 65 or older and eligible for social security retirement benefits. The coverage offered by Medicare is for skilled nursing home care for a *maximum of 20 days* when nursing home residency immediately follows qualified hospitalization. Not every hospital patient qualifies for this coverage. For days 21 through 100, Medicare *pays only a portion* of expenses. After 100 days in a nursing home, Medicare *pays nothing.* Clearly, Medicare is not a readily available source of funds to pay for your long-term care.

Women can't afford, however, to ignore Medicaid rules. Most women will outlive their spouses and may not have the same income when their spouses pass away. A large number of baby-boomer women have elected not to enter the work force, causing them to rely solely on their spouses. If you or your spouse haven't planned well, you may be left with little to no income at your husband's death. Or if you are thinking about caring for an elderly parent, you need to understand Medicaid. Furthermore, a woman in the workforce is generally not thinking about saving for her golden years or for her long-term care. Still, only those in poverty meet the requirements to be eligible for Medicaid. In fact, 80% of widows now living in poverty were not poor before the death of their spouses. Medicaid knowledge is important for all women to understand.

Medicaid (also known as MEDICAL ASSISTANCE in many states), is the only government benefit available to provide money for long-term nursing home care. Medicaid is a joint federal-state program providing medical assistance for persons with very few assets who are aged, blind or disabled. Each state administers its federal Medicaid program according to general standards set by Congress. In order to determine the eligibility of an applicant to receive Medicaid payments for nursing home care, the state's Medicaid department will consider the applicant's income and resources (as well as that of the applicant's spouse) to determine whether or not the applicant qualifies for Medicaid based on financial need.

Medicaid Planning for Nursing Home Costs

MEDICAID

Medicaid is a welfare program intended for those who cannot afford to pay for nursing home care. Because of the increasing cost of such care, many women are interested in arranging their income and assets so that they can qualify for Medicaid and at the same time keep their assets for their family.

WHO CAN QUALIFY FOR MEDICAID?

In order to qualify for Medicaid, you must meet certain requirements based upon residency, financial need and medical need. The office of the aging or similar agency in your city or county will assist with the medical evaluation required for Medicaid. The determination of financial need is administered locally through your city or county welfare assistance office. There are two financial tests to determine if one qualifies financially to receive Medicaid: the Assets Test and the Income Test.

The Assets Test

When one applies for Medicaid, the applicant's assets are reviewed by state Medicaid officials. All of the applicant's assets are divided into one of the two following categories:

- Countable ("available") Assets: These are assets the applicant must use to pay for the cost of care. Everything owned by the applicant is considered a countable asset unless specifically exempted by law.

- Noncountable ("unavailable") Assets: These are assets that the applicant (and the applicant's spouse if married) is permitted to keep and still receive Medicaid payments.

What is the maximum total countable assets an applicant can have and still qualify for Medicaid? This figure varies by state, but it is typically $2,000. If an applicant has more than this amount in countable assets, she will not qualify for Medicaid.

The Community Spouse's Assets

There are some special rules for Medicaid applicants who are married. For example, a portion of the total assets owned by both the spouse living in a nursing home ("institutional spouse") and the spouse living in the community ("community spouse") is legally protected for the use of the community spouse. This portion is called the "protected spousal share" and is not considered a countable asset which must be used to pay for nursing home care. The protected spousal share that the community spouse is entitled to keep is equal to one-half of the value of the total combined assets of the applicant and the community spouse up to a maximum of $92,760 (with the minimum of $18,552). These dollar amounts change every year. This amount is in addition to the $2,000 of countable assets the nursing home spouse is allowed to keep. Once the community spouse is institutionalized, the assets of each are counted separately.

Assets You May Keep and Still Qualify for Medicaid

In considering an applicant's assets, noncountable assets are:

- applicant's personal residence (some states allow this exemption only if you have a spouse or dependent relative living with you in your residence),
- household goods,
- one motor vehicle,
- burial plot and irrevocable burial reserve in a reasonable amount,
- life insurance (whole life with cash value up to a maximum of $1,000 and term policies to any value) and
- assets used in a trade or business essential to self-support.
- The following assets are also exempt if the applicant is married: community spouse's IRA, 401(k), pension funds, Keogh plan and community spouse's "protected spousal share."

For example, your husband enters a nursing home, and together you own the following assets: one car, your home, $11,000 in a bank account in his name only, $9,000 in a bank account in your name only and a life insurance policy with a cash value of $2,000. The Medicaid office finds countable assets totaling $22,000 (both bank accounts plus the life insurance policy). The car and the home are noncountable assets. All of the remaining assets are countable assets whether they are in the name of the institutionalized spouse, your husband, or not. The "protected spousal share" that the wife may keep is one-half of the $22,000 total countable assets or $11,000. Fortunately for her, however, the minimum "protected spousal share" is $18,552, and this is what she may keep. The value of the rest of the countable assets is $3,448 ($22,000 - $18,552). Therefore, as a couple, you must spend $1,448 in order to qualify the husband for Medicaid because he is only allowed to have $2,000 in his name while receiving Medicaid payments. All other countable assets owned by the husband, including jointly owned property, must be transferred out of his name and into your name within 90 days of the initial eligibility determination.

The Income Test

All income of the applicant, except for a $30 per month allowance for personal needs, is considered available to pay for healthcare. This includes income from social security and private pensions as well as any other income including interest and dividends from investments.

The Community Spouse's Income

The community spouse is permitted to have income to live on, known as a minimum monthly maintenance needs allowance (also known as MMMNA). The MMMNA is the minimum amount of income needed to maintain the community spouse at home. This amount changes every year and is currently $1,567 of income per month. In situations where the amount of income earned by the community spouse is *below* the MMMNA amount, the community spouse may receive income from the institutionalized spouse to increase the monthly income of the community spouse to the minimum monthly allowance. This is known as the "income first rule."

In many states, community spouses with incomes below the MMMNA amount have another strategy to increase their incomes. This is to increase the value of the protected spousal share to the amount necessary to produce enough income to equal the MMMNA. The additional amount of the protected spousal share is determined by calculating the value of a commercial annuity that would generate the income necessary to equal the MMMNA amount. In some states, the community spouse is not required to purchase a commercial annuity but is deemed to have the income that would be derived if such an annuity were purchased.

Considerations When Making Gifts to Qualify for Medicaid

Since Medicaid payments are based on need, most of those who do not qualify fail to qualify because they have too many assets. Therefore, many people try to qualify for Medicaid by giving away all of their assets. The practice of giving away assets to qualify for government benefits has caused much discussion concerning the moral and ethical issues it raises. In addition, giving away assets before entering a long-term care facility can reduce your options regarding the type of facility that you enter. Many retirement communities do not depend on government programs, and only those residents who can pay for their services are admitted.

The Look-Back Period

To discourage such gift giving, states require that any asset given away during a "look-back" period must be included as a countable asset that still belongs to the applicant.

The look-back period begins on the day that the applicant is both institutionalized and applies for Medicaid. When one applies for Medicaid, the state looks back three years from the date of application to determine if gifts were made to individuals and five years to see if any gifts were made to or from trusts. If any gifts were made, the applicant will be ineligible to receive Medicaid for a specified period of time.

The period of time that the applicant is denied Medicaid if gifts were made during the look-back period is equal to the number of months of nursing home care the applicant could have paid for using the money that was given away. To calculate this period of time, the state will divide the total value of gifts given by the average monthly rate for nursing home care where you reside. The period of ineligibility begins upon the date of transfer.

If Mother, a resident of Pennsylvania, transferred $100,000 to her children 30 days before she entered a nursing home and applied for Medicaid, she would be denied Medicaid benefits for a period of time equal to $100,000 (the amount of the gift) divided by $5,787.38 (the average monthly rate for private pay nursing home care in Pennsylvania), which equals 17 months of ineligibility for Medicaid.

It is important to understand that the period of time of ineligibility begins to run as of the date of the gift and not the date Mother went into the nursing home. Therefore, if she had made her gift 17 months before she entered the nursing home and applied for Medicaid, she would not have any period of ineligibility due to the $100,000 gift.

Permitted Transfers

Some transfers during the look-back period are permitted. Permitted transfers include any transfer to a spouse or, under limited exceptions, transfers of a residence. If either spouse makes a gift, both can be denied benefits for up to 36 months regardless of which one enters a nursing home.

Transfer Risks

Transferring assets in order to qualify for Medicaid carries with it certain risks. The risks involving transfers are based on the fact that transferred assets are irrevocably owned by the transferee who may squander the assets or lose them in a divorce or bankruptcy. In addition, there are numerous tax traps that must be considered. Clearly, one should retain enough assets to pay for care during any period of ineligibility. Transfers of assets should not be undertaken without legal advice from an attorney who regularly practices in this area of law.

Transfer Strategies

A number of transfer strategies have developed to assist one in qualifying for Medicaid while maximizing the amount of assets passed on to family and heirs. It cannot be overstated that the permissibility of these strategies is subject to change at a moment's notice. This is an *ever-changing* area of law, and a strategy that is acceptable today may be no longer permitted tomorrow. It is important to consult with experienced legal counsel before engaging in any of these strategies.

Medicaid Estate Recovery Program

The appropriate state welfare department in your state of residence is charged with recovering from an individual's probate estate any amounts the state paid for Medicaid on behalf of the decedent during the last five years of his life. The executor is required to send notice to the department to ask whether a claim exists. If the decedent is survived by a spouse living in the house, the department must postpone collection until after his or her death. It is interesting to note that assets held in a REVOCABLE LIVING TRUST are not probate estate assets and are not currently subject to this program. Many departments, however, hold that transfer of a principal residence of applicant or applicant's spouse into a revocable living trust causes it to lose its status as a noncountable asset.

The Use of Trusts in Medicaid Planning

There are no benefits using revocable living trusts when it comes to Medicaid planning. There are a few IRREVOCABLE TRUSTS that can be utilized to protect assets from long-term care costs. Transfer to trusts incur the five-year look-back penalty or must be TESTAMENTARY. Nevertheless, in the right circumstances, irrevocable trusts can be excellent planning tools.

> You should get expert advice as soon as the need for long-term care becomes evident. To delay seeking advice from a qualified professional advisor may result in lost benefits.

Long-Term Care Insurance

Long-term care includes a broad spectrum of care. Long-term care refers to a person residing in a skilled nursing facility receiving 24-hour care under the supervision of a physician. It also refers to a person receiving only custodial care (help with bathing, dressing and eating). Long-term care is care that is needed for long periods of time and is not considered to be rehabilitative. It can be provided in a nursing home setting, in the recipient's own home or in a group setting such as an assisted living facility.

WHO SHOULD CONSIDER LONG-TERM CARE INSURANCE?

Since the prospects of qualifying for Medicaid are not encouraging, a growing number of women are purchasing long-term care insurance. Studies reveal that only about 16% of those age 65 and over have private long-term care insurance. Although this is a small percentage, it is growing quickly. Over eight million long-term care insurance policies were sold in 2001 alone. You must take into account the factors listed on the following pages to determine whether this type of insurance is for you.

Long-term care insurance should also be considered by those women desiring to maintain their independence because it can provide them with the money needed for them to stay at home. In addition, long-term care insurance benefits would permit you to avoid depending upon your children for care and would eliminate financial concerns of a long lifetime. Remember, most women live an average of seven years longer than most men. Long-term care insurance would also permit retaining some inheritance for one's children. Every woman ought to consider the benefits of long-term care insurance.

Goals

You must decide why you would purchase long-term care insurance. It can help you maintain your independence and avoid becoming dependent upon your children or other family members for your care. It can help you avoid receiving government handouts. It can also avoid impoverishing your spouse if you are married and protect your estate for your children or other loved ones. Perhaps most important of all, long-term care insurance increases the possibility of you receiving care at your home and thereby totally avoiding placement in a nursing home or assisted living facility. If your health becomes such that care at home is not possible, long-term care can provide better choices of facilities because many such facilities do not accept residents who cannot pay for their own care.

Risk

You must decide if you face a significant risk of needing long-term care. It has been estimated that among all people who live to age 65, one in three will spend three months or more in a nursing home. About one in four will spend one year or more in a nursing home, and about one in 11 will spend five years or more in a nursing home.

As a woman, you should be aware that your risk of spending an extended time in a nursing home is much greater. This is because of the fact that you have a longer life expectancy and, if you are married, chances are that you will outlive your husband.

Age

According to experts in the field, long-term care insurance can be most beneficial to those between the ages of 55 and 75. Many women in this age group, however, are focused on accumulating assets for retirement and are reluctant to spend the money for a future need they feel they may never have. Nevertheless, this is an ideal age for most women to acquire the coverage because of the lower rates.

Estate Size

Those with estates of between $150,000 and $2 million are good candidates to consider long-term care insurance. Women with estates this size can usually afford to pay the premium. Typically, individuals with estates in this range are planning to use their assets to live on during retirement years and still have something left over to pass to heirs. Those with estates over $2 million may not need long-term care insurance because they would have the income necessary to pay for long-term care if needed. Those women with less than $150,000 may find the premiums to be too high relative to the size of their estates.

For planning purposes, one should presume that it would take a $1 million diversified investment portfolio to produce sufficient income to pay the annual costs of nursing home or home care.

Tax-Qualified Long-Term Care Policies

The federal government has pursued an interest in encouraging taxpayers to purchase long-term care insurance. Policies issued after January 1, 1997, qualify to have the premiums be tax deductible and the benefits be tax free. This tax benefit is only for policies that meet certain standards and are therefore considered "tax-qualified policies."

Long-Term Care Insurance for Women Who Are Federal Employees

In October of 2002, the Long-Term Care Security Act took effect. This law makes special long-term care policies available to federal employees, military personnel and members of the uniformed services. These federal employees and retirees may want to consider the long-term care benefits available through this special program by reviewing the information available from the Office of Personnel Management at www.opm.gov.insure.ltc, or by contacting the National Association of Retired Federal Employees (NARFE) in Alexandria, Va., at (708) 838-7780 or www.narfe.org.

WHAT TO LOOK FOR IN A LONG-TERM CARE INSURANCE POLICY

Levels of Care Covered

The levels of care paid for by the various long-term care insurance companies include nursing home coverage for skilled, intermediate and custodial care. In addition to paying for nursing home expenses, many policies now also provide for home care coverage. Home care coverage should be investigated closely in the contract. If available, it can provide such services as skilled care, adult daycare, home health aides and personal care attendants, all while you stay in your home. Coverage for assisted living care, respite care and inflation protection should also be considered when shopping for long-term care insurance.

Daily Benefit

This is the maximum dollar amount that the insurance company will pay for care each day. The average daily cost of skilled care in the area in which you wish to live in retirement should be used to determine an adequate DAILY BENEFIT.

Elimination Period

This is the number of days that you must pay your own expenses before the insurance company begins paying benefits.

There are no benefits paid during the elimination period (also known as "the waiting period"). Elimination periods typically run from zero to 180 days. The most common periods, however, are generally from 20 to 60 days. The policy premium will be lower with a longer elimination period.

Benefit Period

This is the period of time during which benefits will be paid at the full daily rate. Typical periods are two, three, four, five and six years or lifetime. The longer the benefit period, of course, the more expensive the policy. Considering the expense of coverage, typical guidelines are that if you are under 60 years of age, lifetime coverage would be preferred. For those who are over 80 years of age, many commentators suggest three to five years of coverage. Women between 60 and 80 years of age might want to consider a minimum term of three years with the length of the term dictated by cash resources.

When considering the BENEFIT PERIOD of policies, it is important to consider both long-term care and short-term care. Medicare strictly limits the number of days of coverage for hospitalization and skilled nursing services. The result is that more people are being required to pay for REHABILITATIVE CARE (also known as SHORT-TERM CARE). Long-term care policies that have a RESTORATION OF BENEFITS clause would cover these short-term rehabilitative periods based on such events as stroke or hip fracture.

When you are planning for long-term care, it may also be a good time to consider making funeral arrangements for yourself. Women are often the ones left to do this for others. These arrangements might include anything from buying a grave site to writing out your ideal memorial service commemorating your life. Some funeral services and cemeteries offer prepaid plans and preplanned choices. All these decisions go into estate planning and make it easier on loved ones.

The costs of long-term care, whether in a nursing home or at your home, are expected to continue to rise significantly. Any woman who wants a comprehensive approach to estate planning should give serious consideration to long-term care insurance. The options are so wide ranging that you should be able to custom fit coverage to your specific needs and desires. Married couples should invest in coverage for both spouses. Before purchasing long-term care insurance, it is important to work with a professional advisor experienced in this area.

Trusts for Family Members With Disabilities

One of the more serious concerns facing the parents of a disabled child is knowing who will care for their child after the parents die or become incapacitated. A significant number of families face this unique challenge. A study by the University of Illinois at Chicago revealed that nearly 500,000 disabled adults live with at least one parent who is at least 60 years old. Unfortunately, many of these parents do not know who will care for their disabled child after they are gone. Providing financial stability for such children is fairly easy for parents who have the resources, but providing *personal* care for such children may be a challenge. Parents whose resources may already be depleted after many years of caring for their child face both the financial and the practical issues. In some cases, siblings will step in to continue to care for the disabled child, but often families must depend on government benefits to take care of them. Some disabled children who receive government benefits to take care of them may lose their eligibility for those benefits if they receive any sort of inheritance. In such situations, a unique type of trust for special needs may be very helpful.

WHAT ARE SPECIAL NEEDS TRUSTS AND SUPPLEMENTAL NEEDS TRUSTS?

Experts predict that one of the most significant growth areas of elder law in the coming years will deal with two types of trusts, the special needs trust and the supplemental needs trust. Before a discussion of these trusts can be undertaken, it is important to comment upon the confusing language surrounding these trusts. Despite their similar names, experts generally differentiate between a supplemental needs trust and a special needs trust.

A special needs trust is created by a family member or other person for the benefit of a disabled beneficiary using the beneficiary's own money. In order to receive distributions from the trust and also continue the beneficiary's eligibility for government benefits, a special needs trust is used to hold the beneficiary's money. These trusts provide that, upon the death of the disabled beneficiary, the trust must reimburse the state for any Medicaid benefits it has paid to the disabled beneficiary before any other trust beneficiaries can receive trust distributions. Based on the federal law that permits such trusts, they are also known as "(d)(4)(A)" trusts.

When a special needs trust is established for a disabled individual using the disabled individual's own funds, it is frequently the result of a lawsuit recovery or settlement, or the disabled individual is a beneficiary of an estate or insurance policy.

The supplemental needs trust, like the special needs trust, is established to protect the beneficiary's eligibility to receive government benefits. Supplemental needs trusts, however, are established by people who are not concerned about qualifying for government benefits themselves and who use their own money to fund the trust, not money that belongs to the disabled person. Since the person establishing the supplemental needs trust has no need for government benefits, a supplemental needs trust is permitted to distribute the remainder of the trust to beneficiaries after the death of the disabled beneficiary, without regard for reimbursement to the state for any Medicaid payments received by the disabled beneficiary.

Since this book is intended as an estate planning guide, the following discussion will focus on the supplemental needs trust and will not include further discussions regarding the special needs trust.

The Benefits of a Supplemental Needs Trust

The supplemental needs trust has been developed in answer to the challenge that many families face in not being able to afford to provide for all of the needs of a disabled child. When faced with these expenses, parents will often utilize the services and benefits available from federal, state and local government programs. This allows the families to maintain family resources in case government programs would no longer be available for the child. Since many government benefits are paid only to needy recipients, a benefit of the supplemental needs trust is that it provides funds to supplement (but not supplant) the care provided by government benefits for the disabled child, and yet does not limit the ability of the child to receive government benefits.

THE SUPPLEMENTAL NEEDS TRUST

Estate planning for families with a child with disabilities requires special attention. One challenge is to provide benefits from the estate of the parents while at the same time ensuring no loss of government benefits to their disabled son or daughter. Another major concern of the parents is the question of who will take care of their child once they are gone. A supplemental needs trust is a trust arrangement established by parents (or others) to provide an inheritance for their disabled child to pay for his or her care and not have that inheritance diminish any government benefits available to the child.

How Supplemental Needs Trusts Are Established

A supplemental needs trust may be established in the will or living trust of the parents or in a separate supplemental needs trust document. The supplemental needs trust permits trust distributions for expenses not covered by government benefits such as education, training and rehabilitation, companions or nursing aid services, recreation, entertainment and travel expenses.

The supplemental needs language must be carefully worded so that the principal and income of the trust is not permitted to be used for any benefit that could be paid for by government benefits. If the trust is not written correctly, the government benefits will be denied until the trust is completely used up.

Who Should Be Trustee?

The selection of trustee of a supplemental needs trust is of special importance. The trustee has two broad functions:

1. Administer the trust assets relating to investment management decisions, tax reporting and gathering the income.

2. Determine the amount and payee of distributions that need to be made to or for the benefit of the disabled child.
   The trustee should not only be knowledgeable about the needs of the child, but also experienced in financial management. The pairing of a family member with a corporate trustee as co-trustees is a good combination for such trusts. The corporate trustee would manage the trust

and its investments, and the family member would make the decisions regarding spending trust assets for the benefit of the disabled child. The individual family member co-trustee could also have the authority to change the corporate trustee, as well as the authority to hire experts.

Elements Required in a Supplemental Needs Trust
(established in a will or revocable living trust)

It is important that a number of factors be clearly addressed in a supplemental needs trust. The law relating to supplemental needs trusts is constantly evolving. It is critical to consult with an attorney experienced with this very unique area of the law.

- The trust must clearly state that it is to "supplement, but not supplant, government benefits to which the child may otherwise be entitled."

- The trust must specify that the grantor's intent is that after the death of the disabled child, specific individuals will receive the remainder in the trust, usually the siblings of the disabled child.

- The trust should identify the benefits that the disabled child is receiving or would be qualified to receive.

- The trust must not provide for distributions directly to the disabled child.

- The trust should give the trustee the authority to spend or accumulate income in the trustee's sole discretion.

- The trust should clearly identify the state and its agencies as creditors prohibited from receiving distributions from the trust.

- The trust should have a spendthrift clause preventing the child from pledging trust assets as collateral for loans and preventing any creditors from acquiring trust assets.

How Supplemental Needs Trusts Operate

After the death of the one who established the trust (or immediately if the trust was funded during the grantor's lifetime), the trustee may distribute income and/or principal for the benefit of the child with the restriction that such distributions may only supplement and not replace government benefits to which the child is entitled. Upon the death of the child, the remaining trust assets must be payable to individuals other than the child's estate; this is usually the child's siblings. A supplemental needs trust is often named as the beneficiary of a life insurance policy that the parents may purchase on their own lives. This is a strategy employed to assure that the trust will have enough assets to care for the disabled child after the parents are gone.

Summary

There are many considerations to staying in control of your assets as you age and as you move through the seasons of life. Hopefully this chapter has persuaded you that it is important to plan for possible incapacity. In the event of your incapacity, your needs fall into one of two broad categories — either managing your finances or your healthcare requirements. You must be sure that you have identified the people that you want to handle your affairs. Although none of us can predict the future, there is a strong possibility that you or your spouse will eventually require skilled nursing care — either at home or in a nursing home.

Women need to make these plans for themselves in advance. And because many men tend to avoid these difficult issues, women in their lives can help them and others to take into consideration the need for such planning. Planning for these costs now can greatly minimize the impact upon your estate. Planning for other family members that have disabilities is also an issue of critical importance to the women who care for those family members now.

Step 5

Control the Distribution of Your Assets After Death, Divorce, Remarriage or Widowhood

Topics Include

The Nine Benefits of Wills

Choosing Your Executor

Various Types of Trusts

Divorce Considerations

Remarriage and Single Parenting Considerations

Widowhood and Special Considerations

Settling a Trust Estate

Introduction

*I*F YOU'VE READ THE EARLIER CHAPTERS, and not skipped ahead, you know that you must approach estate planning with a knowledgeable team; then, you must ensure that your nonprobate assets have beneficiary designations that align in practical terms with your will. Also, you understand the various types of ownership and what each means in terms of inheritance, and you have considered the various issues surrounding incapacity. Now, on to the finer points of creating your will and the pros and cons of trusts and creating a trust as the primary estate planning vehicle. Most importantly, this chapter focuses on concerns that are both critical and unique to women.

Your Will

A will is a unique legal document in that it does not become legally binding until the person who signed it dies. A chief purpose of a will is to communicate the wishes of the signer (TESTATOR for men and TESTATRIX for women) as to distribution of her assets upon death. Wills can be revoked by the testator at any time by destroying the original document. The terms of an existing will can be modified by using a simple amendment known as a CODICIL. Whenever you have a new will prepared, the new will states that it revokes the prior will. The will with the most recent date is the one that is legal.

The will is the estate planning document that generally gets the most attention. Since assets can also pass at death by beneficiary designation, joint ownership, operation of law and trusts (collectively known as will substitutes), a will is only one of many means of controlling asset transfer at death. The explosive growth of annuities, IRAs and retirement plans which pass by beneficiary designation creates the likelihood that even fewer assets will be controlled by wills in the future.

What Makes It Legal?

Intent

In order for a document to be considered a valid will, it must state that the one signing it intends it to be her will, and it must clearly dispose of her assets at death.

CAPACITY

Even if the will is properly signed, there are two other requirements. One is that the person who signed it must be over 18 years of age when it was signed. A second requirement is that the signer must have a sound mind when she signs it.

Being of Sound Mind ...

Although many states have very specific rules, generally one is considered to have the mental capacity to sign a will if she can meet four requirements: (1) she can identify her family members, (2) she has a basic understanding of the assets and possessions she owns, (3) she is able to form a plan for the distribution of her assets and (4) she understands the scope and meaning of the provisions of her will.

SIGNATURE

In many states, the law simply states that every will must be in writing and signed at the end of the document. It is important to have witnesses present who will also sign the will to ensure that the will can withstand possible challenges. These simple rules can be deceiving, and you should always consult a qualified estate planning attorney for assistance.

Many states' laws permit the execution of a self-proving affidavit to prove the will is valid. The person signing the will does so in the presence of two witnesses. The two witnesses also sign the will, stating that they were present when the will was signed and that the signer was over 18 years of age, had a sound mind and was not under duress. Once all three people have signed the will, each signs an affidavit testifying to these conditions, and all signatures are then notarized. The benefit of the self-proving affidavit accompanying the will is that the witnesses will not be required to appear at probate court. If your will does not have this self-proving affidavit attached to it, the witnesses will have to be found after you pass away. After being located, each witness will have to sign a statement that they were present when you signed your will and that the signature is yours. Jurisdictions vary regarding additional requirements for witnesses, procedures for executing a will or exceptions to general rules. Remember that estate planning rules vary among the 50 states and are almost certainly different in other nations.

The Nine Primary Benefits of Wills

Although the importance of the will has diminished in recent years because of the increased availability of other methods to distribute assets at death, a will provides benefits that make it the cornerstone of most estate plans. What follows are the nine primary benefits of wills.

1. CONTROL WHO RECEIVES YOUR ASSETS AFTER DEATH

Your will controls only those assets that are titled in your name alone. These assets are known as your PROBATE ESTATE. Having a will which directs where your assets will go after death means that your estate is "testate." This is because you have written down your desires. To have no will means that your estate is "intestate." That means there is no writing stating your desires about the assets that were in your name alone. Assets in an intestate estate will be distributed according to state law, which could result in distributions to people you may not even know. Intestacy can also cause confusion and conflict among family members, since money and family can be a volatile combination. Adding that stress to the emotion of losing a loved one is certainly something you can plan to avoid.

Proper planning with a will helps assure security for a surviving spouse, parent or children. By leaving an orderly plan of distribution through your will, you can be assured that your heirs will receive your assets according to your desires. Blended families that include children from a previous marriage especially benefit from this type of planning, which can ensure that everything is considered and no one is left out. Also, if you have no will, there will be no gifts to your favorite charities.

2. NAME YOUR OWN PERSONAL REPRESENTATIVE (EXECUTOR)

A will permits you to name the individual or institution you wish to carry out your instructions after death. This person or institution is your PERSONAL REPRESENTATIVE. (Historically the term was EXECUTRIX for women and EXECUTOR for men.)

Responsibilities of a Personal Representative After the Death of the One Making the Will

1. Locate the will. (Make her job easier by telling her that she is the personal representative and where your will is located.)

2. Present the will to the probate court at the city or county courthouse.

3. Locate and conserve assets (i.e., house, bank accounts, personal belongings, business, etc.). Note: Nonprobate assets such as life insurance policies, 401(k) accounts and IRAs are not the responsibility of the personal representative.

4. Notify creditors and pay the debts and any claims against the estate.

5. File the decedent's final income tax return and pay any taxes due.

6. Distribute the assets according to the will.

When choosing your personal representative, keep in mind that it can be one or more persons, a bank or a trust company. A number of considerations apply when choosing the personal representative. The primary one should be the ability to do the job. Personal representatives generally hire an attorney to assist them; therefore, their skill may not be as important as their trustworthiness. Typically, a husband and wife name each other as the personal representative and then name either adult children, a bank or a trust company as the successor personal representative. There are a number of advantages to naming a bank or a trust company as a personal representative (discussed later in Step 5).

The personal representative is entitled to receive compensation for her services. Typically, laws state that compensation to the personal representative shall be "reasonable."

If you are named the personal representative in someone else's will, keep in mind that you are not required to hire the attorney who wrote the will to assist you with estate settlement. As personal representative, you should use the attorney that you believe will best serve the estate. This attorney may or may not be the one who wrote the will.

Failure to name a personal representative will result in the court appointing an administrator to manage your estate. The administrator may be an individual or institution that you never used or met during your lifetime. Since you have the right to name an individual, a bank or a trust company to act as your personal representative, it is to your advantage to have a will prepared to do so.

---

3. NAME THE GUARDIAN FOR YOUR MINOR CHILDREN

State laws permit the sole surviving parent of an unmarried minor child to appoint a GUARDIAN OF THE PERSON of such child to care for her until she reaches age 18. A guardian of the person is the individual responsible for the day-to-day care of minor children, such as providing them with food, clothing, shelter and healthcare. Failure of a parent to name a guardian of the person results in the court appointing the guardian. Family conflict could arise as numerous individuals may combat each other for the right to take care of the child. This would incur additional legal costs for the process of having the court appoint a guardian, taking valuable estate resources away from the child.

You may appoint different guardians: one to care for your children (guardian of the person) and another to manage their money (GUARDIAN OF THE ESTATE or "conservator" in many states). For example, you could name your sister as guardian over the care of your children and your father as conservator to manage their money. Take the initiative to name those individuals in your will who you prefer to care for the day-to-day needs of your minor children, and you'll enjoy the peace of mind that results.

4. CONTROL WHEN YOUR CHILDREN, GRANDCHILDREN OR OTHER HEIRS WILL RECEIVE THEIR INHERITANCE

As described in the preceding section, when a child under age 18 receives an inheritance and there is no provision made in a will or trust for its management, the court will determine how the inheritance will be managed. This means that money can only be withdrawn from the account with a court order which costs additional time and money. Upon the minor's 18th birthday, the account will be closed and the minor will receive the entire inheritance. In the case of large estates, another option may be for the court to appoint a guardian of the estate.

The Wisdom of Timing

Grandma Wilson founded a very successful chain of clothing stores, which she led with success and fanfare for 40 years. She then sold the business and decided to create a trust in her will to ensure money was there for the education and support of her grandchildren. She didn't want her daughter or her daughter's husband to have control of this fund. Nor did she want the inheritance to be handed to her grandchildren on their 18th birthdays. Grandma Wilson understood the meaning "easy come, easy go," and she had some specific ideas about how her grandchildren should use their inheritance.

So, in her will she specified that granddaughter Emily would receive $50,000 in trust to be used for college. If Emily decides she suddenly doesn't like the idea of higher education, the $50,000 would be held in trust until her 30th birthday at which time it would be dispersed in installments of $5,000 annually for as long as the assets lasted (as they would be invested to earn interest).

Grandma Wilson's grandson, Mark, was also to receive $50,000. Mark received a scholarship and didn't need money for college. His grandmother thought he might be good in business for himself, so she specified that Mark could use $25,000 of the total to start a business at age 30, with the remaining $25,000 allotted to him in annual payments. If he did not want to start a business, then he would receive the $50,000 in annual $5,000 payments like his sister.

5. PROTECT YOUR HEIRS' INHERITANCE FROM OTHERS

A will provides the flexibility to distribute your estate immediately to your heirs or maintain control by distributing it over a period of time through trusts written within your will. By maintaining your heirs' inheritance in trust, you can protect it in the event of their bankruptcy, lawsuits and divorce settlements. There are different types of trusts, and not all trusts are protected from such lawsuits, but appropriate provisions may be placed in a trust to work to ensure your wishes. Always seek the advice of your estate planning advisor to determine what is best for your situation.

Let's say Emily, in the previous example, does not go to college, but takes the $5,000 per year amount from the trust. By age 40, Emily is on her second marriage when she becomes the victim of a crime and dies. Now, Grandma never intended for Husband Number Two to become the recipient of $5,000 per year for the rest of his life, and fortunately she made the appropriate provisions in her will. The will directs that the money held in trust for Emily reverts to her brother Mark, who decides to fund a rose garden at the local park in his sister's honor because she loved flowers and this was something Mark could do in her memory. Husband Number Two was surprised as he quickly learned the nuances of women in establishing their own estate plans.

6. TURN TAX DOLLARS INTO FAMILY DOLLARS

By using tax strategies in your will, you can save a significant portion of your estate from federal taxes. Step 8 discusses estate taxes and gives specific directions outlining how to achieve these tax savings. Using proper tax strategies can allow more money to pass to your beneficiaries. All women would rather see their money pass to loved ones than to any state or federal government treasury. That is not possible unless you have a will.

7. GIVE GIFTS TO SPECIAL PEOPLE AND CHARITIES

Americans contribute billions of dollars each year to charities. When planning their estates, however, they may overlook the fact that without a will, there are no distributions made to charities or anyone outside of one's family according to state laws that govern if one dies without a will. This can mean a substantial loss of funds to close friends or charities.

If you contribute to the support of charities or special individuals during your lifetime, be sure to consider them when creating your will. Otherwise, they may be left with nothing after you pass away. The beauty of giving gifts to charities is that they go on perpetually, and a portion of your estate can continue to make a difference even after you are gone. In addition, gifts to charities made through your will result in inheritance and estate tax deductions.

8. PROTECT GOVERNMENT BENEFITS OF FAMILY MEMBERS WITH DISABILITIES

Many families have children with disabilities that cause the child to be dependent on others for assistance during their adult lives. While their parents are living, such a child could live with them. Upon the death of the surviving parent, however, such children may require residential or nursing home services.

If a parent or grandparent leaves an inheritance outright to a disabled child, the child would be required to fully consume his or her entire inheritance before qualifying for certain government benefits. With proper planning inside their wills, the parents can make financial provision for such a child, while permitting him or her to continue to receive government benefits.

9. DETERMINE WHO MUST PAY THE INHERITANCE TAX

An inheritance tax is a tax on an heir who inherits something. Some states assess this tax, while others do not, but when it is assessed, it is critical. (It is important to ask your attorney if your state does assess an inheritance tax. For example, New Jersey does have a tax on inheritances while New York does not.)

As mentioned earlier, quite often a woman's will might state that any taxes due from her estate should be paid from the probate estate as an expense of administration. (The probate estate is the one portion of your total estate that is controlled by your will.)

There are many assets, however, (i.e. annuities, life insurance, T.O.D. accounts) that pass outside your will and are known as NONPROBATE ASSETS. If your will specifies that all taxes are to be paid from your probate estate, then any inheritance tax due upon annuities and IRAs received by your heirs will be paid from the portion of your estate going to the heirs named in your will. As a result, those receiving the distribution as a nonprobate asset are not required to pay the inheritance tax on the portion of your estate that they inherit, since the tax will not be deducted from the annuities or IRAs. The residual beneficiaries of the will must have this tax deducted from their inheritance.

It is not unusual for the beneficiaries named in a will to be surprised to discover that nonprobate assets (IRAs or annuities, for example) have been distributed to someone else. This can result in anything from mild annoyance to definite hardship on the part of the beneficiary of the will. The incorrect use of tax language in wills contributes to confusion and conflict. This is especially the case when the estate has a substantial amount of nonprobate assets that pass to the beneficiaries, while those who receive their inheritance under the will are saddled with paying the full amount of tax on the nonprobate assets.

The Disadvantages of Wills

In spite of the nine primary benefits that wills provide, there are two disadvantages: (1) A will controls only those assets in your sole name. This means that the plans so carefully laid out in your will cannot control nonprobate assets such as your IRAs or annuities. (2) Since your will only controls your assets after your death, it has no control over your assets if you become incapacitated.

Introduction to Living Trusts

Living trusts may be the most misunderstood of all estate planning documents. They are sold by telemarketers, direct mail, seminars and door-to-door salesmen. Unfortunately, this mass-marketing approach has resulted in more misunderstanding about living trusts than positive education. Wise women understand the need for good counsel in this area (and don't want to just take the advice of their hairdressers!).

The role of the attorney on the estate planning team — one who is knowledgeable about living trusts — is critical when it comes to preparing living trusts. You are well advised to secure the assistance of an attorney for the preparation of legal documents that affect your assets.

It is possible that a living trust is not to your advantage. There are many circumstances in which a well-crafted will and durable power of attorney will be sufficient, but only a qualified attorney should advise you on this matter. A trust does not replace a will, does not serve as a tax shelter and may or may not shelter your assets from creditors. They do, however, offer several advantages that women should know.

Trusts

Taking the time and effort to establish a trust can relieve the anxiety you might feel when considering what would happen to your children, elderly parents, spouse or disabled children should you become incapacitated or upon your passing. Therefore, it is wise and responsible to make decisions now that will keep everything running smoothly if the unforeseen happens.

What Is a Trust?

Assume that you are going on an extended trip and want to give your daughter $1,000 to help her with her living needs. You could simply write a check and hand it to her. If you are uncomfortable with just handing her the money and want to have some strings attached to it, you could give the money to your brother instead of directly to your daughter. You would give your brother instructions concerning how the money should be used to benefit your daughter. For example, you could write him a note and tell him that he can use the money to help pay for her rent or medical bills. You would not want him to give it to her so she could buy 20 pairs of shoes.

Instead of giving the money directly to her, you have established a TRUST by giving the $1,000 to your brother to manage for your daughter's benefit. You are the GRANTOR because you are the one that gave the money to your brother. Your brother is the TRUSTEE because he is the one responsible to manage and distribute the money for your daughter's benefit. Your daughter is the trust BENEFICIARY because she is the one who receives the benefits of the money that is held in trust. The note you wrote to your brother is the TRUST AGREEMENT. This is the set of instructions that the grantor (you) desires for the management of the money given to the trustee (your brother). The assets transferred into the trust are known as the PRINCIPAL of the trust. The benefit to you is that you set the guidelines and restrictions on use of the money.

All trusts fall into one or more of the following categories: IRREVOCABLE or REVOCABLE, and LIVING or TESTAMENTARY. If a trust is established during the grantor's lifetime, it is known as a living trust. It will be either revocable or irrevocable. If a trust is established after the grantor's death, it is known as a TESTAMENTARY TRUST.

TESTAMENTARY TRUSTS

Although a trust may be designed and written during the grantor's lifetime (in a will for example), the plan may be that it is not established and funded until after the death of the grantor. This type of trust is a testamentary trust. Since these trusts do not exist until the death of the grantor, they are always irrevocable once your will is probated but can be changed prior to the grantor's death. Furthermore, once established and properly executed, a will is not final and effective until the death of the testator. Testamentary trusts are usually written into the grantor's will or living trust and are established to provide investment management and control over the distribution of trust assets.

IRREVOCABLE TRUSTS

If the grantor decides to give up the right to revoke or amend the trust, he has established an irrevocable trust. These trusts are like lobster traps in that once the assets are put into the trust, they can never come back out. The primary reason that one would establish an irrevocable trust is to provide estate, income or gift tax benefits to the grantor. Irrevocable trusts must have their own tax identification number and may be required to file tax returns. Your estate planning advisor can assist you in deciding if an irrevocable trust is an appropriate avenue for your estate plan.

REVOCABLE LIVING TRUSTS

The distinguishing characteristic of a revocable living trust (RTL) is that the grantor reserves the right to amend or revoke the trust at any time. This type of trust is also known for income tax purposes as a GRANTOR TRUST. This is because the IRS assigns the grantor's own social security number as the tax ID number of the trust as long as the grantor is also serving as the trustee. Hence, there is no requirement for a separate income tax return for the trust, so long as the grantor serves as the trustee and the trust is revocable. In such a trust, the person creating the trust can reserve the right to change it and still has control over many things during his or her lifetime. Your estate planning advisor can assist you in deciding if a revocable trust is an appropriate avenue for your estate plan.

A revocable living trust is a legal document designed, created and signed by you while you are alive, hence the word "living." It is revocable because you are reserving the power to revoke it at any time. You are also creating options and opportunities for yourself with a revocable living trust. You may choose to fund it now, later or periodically as you are able. It is really a wonderful way for any woman who owns real estate assets in more than one state, or holds assets jointly with her spouse.

Women sometimes "just go along" with the husband's creative idea of estate planning, which is likely based on his perspective, not necessarily hers, and is often based on his survival and that of the marriage. An estate planning advisor will want to be concerned for past divorces, blended families, inheritances and marital agreements. Customized trusts can solve many of these dilemmas.

Trusts can avoid many difficulties, such as the use of pre-marital agreements, spendthrift spouse concerns and individuals moving from one state to another with different estate planning rules. Provisions covering these and other concerns can be written into revocable living trusts.

The Eight Primary Benefits of Living Trusts

1. A Living Trust-Centered Estate Plan Creates a Master Plan to Control the Distribution of All Your Assets Upon Your Death

Envision for a moment a wagon wheel, spokes extending outward. If the wheel represents your estate plan, with the spokes the various assets (your home, annuities, life insurance, etc.), then the hub represents your living trust. A living trust is the hub of your estate plan, and all assets and property are brought under the control of one managing document — a document that is able to operate seamlessly beyond your lifetime. With the living trust-centered estate plan, all of your assets and property are brought into one master plan since the living trust sweeps all probate and most nonprobate assets under the authority of just one document.

A living trust ensures continuity among the various assets of your estate and how they are handled. Instead of assets being distributed by different plans set up at different times by different advisors, the living trust provides one comprehensive estate plan for the management and distribution of all your assets.

Along with your living trust, your attorney will have you sign a pour-over will. This will ensures that any assets not in your trust at the time of your death will "pour over" into your trust to be distributed, assuring that your plans are carried out in an orderly, secure manner.

Living trusts can ensure that life insurance proceeds are handled exactly as you wish; they can also prevent accidental disinheritance, a result of joint ownership discussed in Step 3. In short, the directions in the trust may be tailored to meet the specific needs of your loved ones.

Another benefit of living trusts is that investments registered as T.O.D. (transfer on death) or P.O.D. (payable on death) can also be paid directly to your living trust to be a part of your comprehensive estate plan and still avoid probate.

Life insurance proceeds (not payable to the estate) are non-probate assets, and as such, are not controlled by your will. They are paid directly from the insurance company to the beneficiary named in the policy. By establishing a living trust during your lifetime (and directing that the life insurance benefits be paid to the trustee of your revocable living trust), the proceeds will be fully controlled by your trust after death and still avoid probate. This arrangement permits you to pay the proceeds outright to your loved ones or to have the proceeds managed for their benefit. The living trust affords the opportunity for you to address the needs of your family in a more personal manner.

Understanding trusts opens up other alternatives for your estate plan as well. You may want to consider the use of an irrevocable life insurance trust in place of having insurance proceeds paid to the revocable living trust. This can help avoid the incidents of ownership of a large insurance policy. A life insurance trust can distribute assets in the same way that the revocable living trust directs and may be more helpful to you depending on your circumstances.

Most major financial firms (such as Fidelity, Prudential, Schwab, etc.) have simplified the transfers to a revocable living trust by having their own forms and instructions available online. Using and transferring assets into a trust may be easier than most women think.

Barbara was the successful owner of an investment company. A hands-on entrepreneur, she managed the firm's largest portfolios, and her attention to her business was nonstop.

One unfortunate evening, she was involved in a car accident. She survived but sustained a severe concussion, and her legs suffered extensive trauma. She would return to her business, but the rehabilitation was going to be lengthy. Barbara's family, employees and clients were depending on her, but she had to concentrate on getting well.

Fortunately, the previous year Barbara had taken the time to establish a living trust as part of her estate plan. The successor trustee Barbara chose was her father, who had been her mentor and was now retired. Barbara's dad was legally able to step in and manage his daughter's financial affairs while Barbara and her family concentrated on recovery.

---

2. A Living Trust Avoids Court Control of Your Assets in Case of Incapacity

One reason many people establish an estate plan, particularly women, is to confirm the control of their assets if they become incapacitated. A living trust addresses this issue by naming a SUCCESSOR TRUSTEE. If a living trust is in place, with a successor trustee named, then there is no need for the court to appoint a guardian to control your assets if you become incapacitated. Not only will the court not control the management of your assets, but your instructions in the living trust will prevail.

Your living trust continues to control your assets if you become incapacitated because the living trust owns the assets, not you.

What About Your Power of Attorney?

Although the agent you named in your power of attorney has authority to act on your behalf if you become incapacitated, your agent is not required to act. Your successor trustee, however, has a duty to act for your benefit. In addition, the power of attorney may not contain specific instructions regarding your individual desires. The power of attorney contains a list of activities that the agent has your permission to engage in, but it cannot elaborate all of your intentions for yourself and your loved ones. The trustee of your living trust does have specific instructions from you so he or she knows exactly what to do to fulfill your desires. It is important to keep in mind that even those with living trusts should always also have a power of attorney. It will be required to manage assets not held by the trust.

3. A LIVING TRUST SAVES TIME AND MONEY WHEN SETTLING YOUR ESTATE

Assets registered in the name of your living trust are not probate assets and therefore avoid court administration. It is often less costly to settle your estate when your assets are registered in the name of a living trust. This is because you register your assets in the name of your living trust during your lifetime which simplifies the distribution process at your death. Your heirs need not wait for your executor to reregister and transfer the assets. Registering assets in the name of your trust during lifetime should result in lower attorney's fees after death and will also avoid executor's fees. It is important to realize, however, that your successor trustee must have the knowledge and ability to administer your trust and distribute your assets. In the absence of such knowledge, the successor trustee will need to hire the services of a lawyer or CPA to help finalize your affairs. Give careful consideration to your selection of a successor trustee.

We've heard more inaccuracies about trusts, and you may have too. You may have read that there will be no last expenses if you use a living trust, but this is not true. Even with a living trust, there may still be the need to file estate tax returns and a final income tax return. There may also be expenses such as appraisals related to the value of real estate and other assets which must be included in death tax returns.

Assets registered in the name of a living trust can usually be transferred to the beneficiaries after the grantor's death faster than if the assets were to pass through probate. The beauty of a trust is that the successor trustee has immediate access to living trust assets because the successor trustee does not have to engage in the activity of locating your will, probating it and petitioning the probate court to issue a certificate of qualification, all the formalities required to probate a will.

A living trust generally avoids taxation of assets for state probate taxes and may help avoid probate proceedings in other states as well. Real estate owned outside your state of residency is subject to the probate laws of that state. For example, if you lived in Pennsylvania and owned shore property in New Jersey, the state of New Jersey will require probate proceedings to transfer the ownership of that property to the name of your heirs. If you retitled your property into the name of your living trust, it would not be required to go through New Jersey probate, although it may require payment of New Jersey inheritance tax.

4. A LIVING TRUST PROVIDES LIFETIME MANAGEMENT OF YOUR ASSETS

A living trust provides standby professional investment management in the event of your incapacity or prolonged absence. A STANDBY LIVING TRUST is established by naming a bank or trust company as your successor trustee. In such a case, if you leave the country for extended travel or should become incapacitated, you know that there will be continuity in the management of your assets. Also, unlike the power of attorney, the management will be according to your specific directions. Using a standby living trust provides greater assurance that your investments will be professionally managed by the bank or trust company you named until you regain capacity or return to the country. A trust can just plain make a woman's life easier.

5. A LIVING TRUST PROVIDES CONTINUITY OF ASSET MANAGEMENT

Another benefit of living trusts is the continuity they offer upon your death. Remember, although you may (and should) include a power of attorney in your estate plan, this power ends at your death. When probate of estate assets is necessary, assets are frozen until a personal representative (executor) is appointed and a certificate is issued by the probate court. The certificate provides the personal representative the authority to manage your assets. Since a living trust continues after your death, no such freezing is required. As a result, your investments may continue to be actively managed as they were during your lifetime.

Another benefit of continuity is that your successor trustee often has access to your trust assets quicker than the personal representative would have authority over assets in your name alone. The holistic advantage of the living trust is vital to women's lives.

If federal estate tax planning is a part of your estate plan, establishing a living trust assures that assets are transferred into the credit shelter trust of the first spouse to die. If separate (husband and wife) trusts are used, certain assets can be funded solely to one account to simplify future distributions such as the business interest to one child and cash or equivalents to another child who plays no role in the business. Once your living trust is established, it is important to register into the name of the living trust the assets that are planned to become a part of the credit shelter trust after your death. The benefit is that your successor trustee will not be required to make any changes to your investments and could automatically become the trustee of your credit shelter trust. The credit shelter trustee will, however, be required to have a new IRS tax ID number assigned to the credit shelter trust.

6. A LIVING TRUST CAN CONTROL THE TIMING OF THE DISTRIBUTION OF BENEFITS

Women, particularly mothers, spend most of their lives teaching children to think ahead. A trust can carry out that teaching even after you are gone. Your living trust may direct that it pays out to all your beneficiaries immediately upon your death. You also have the option to control the timing of distributions to your heirs. Parents often desire that children receive their inheritance over a number of years — for example, one-third at age 21, one-third at age 25 and the balance at age 30. The successor trustee, under such a plan, would continue to manage the trust assets and make distributions to your heirs over the period of years you specify in your trust.

7. A LIVING TRUST REDUCES THE RISK OF A LAWSUIT

Have you been a peacemaker in your family for a good part of your life? Many women are. A trust can allow you to continue that role even after your passing. Family conflict may be minimized by providing specific instructions in your living trust concerning your assets. This is an excellent way to plan your estate if you suspect there may be some family conflict after you are gone.

Living trusts are more difficult to overturn than wills. Will contests are frequently based upon allegations of mental confusion on the part of the testator. Was she incapacitated? Was she under duress? With a trust those family arguments and questions may be legally irrelevant. One major distinction between a will and a living trust is that the enforceability of a living trust is not totally dependent upon the grantor's state of mind at the time the trust was signed. Since a living trust becomes legally binding when it is signed and is used over time after it is signed, it is far more difficult to overturn. A living trust, by its very nature, shows careful consideration on the part of grantor; registering assets into the name of your trust is additional evidence that you had all your capacities at the time you signed your trust.

8. A Living Trust Provides More Privacy Than Probate

Everyone's will is open to public inspection after death because wills get recorded in the county records office upon probate. When newspapers report the gifts made to charities from estates, it is the result of a reporter reading wills at the courthouse. A living trust is not a public document filed at the courthouse. As a result, the trust is not available to the public.

Although retitling real estate assets is generally done with a transfer deed that must be recorded in the county records office, many states allow retitling of real estate with a more private document that also transfers the assets without recordation tax or grantor's tax so long as the proper code section is listed. The same can be done with high-value personal property, and the transfer document is generally nothing more than a listing of such assets.

Unfortunately, in many states, the state estate tax or inheritance tax return is subject to public review. In spite of this, there is some added privacy with a living trust. These tax returns do not indicate the exact timing of distributions to heirs. In addition, other personal family information in a living trust is not open to public review.

The Parties to a Revocable Living Trust

The person who creates the living trust is known as the GRANTOR. The grantor transfers assets to the trustee of the trust to be controlled by the trustee. The TRUSTEE is named by the grantor when the living trust is established. The grantor usually names herself as the original trustee and manages living trust assets for her own benefit and the benefit of others according to the instructions in the trust agreement. If the grantor has not named herself the trustee, the living trust permits the original trustee to be removed and replaced by the grantor as long as the grantor is alive and not incapacitated.

The SUCCESSOR TRUSTEE continues to manage the living trust assets if the original trustee dies, resigns or becomes incapacitated. The primary BENEFICIARY of a living trust is usually the grantor. Upon the death of the grantor, the successor trustee assumes management authority. The living trust usually directs that upon the death of the grantor, the trust assets should be distributed to the beneficiaries named in the trust agreement.

How to Choose a Trustee

A trustee has a number of duties, assigned to her by law. The trustee must follow the directions written in the living trust by the grantor and is responsible to manage the trust assets according to the terms of the trust. The trustee also has a duty of loyalty to the trust and to the grantor. This means that the trustee cannot act in any way to harm the trust assets or grantor.

Duties of the Trustee

- Collect and control trust assets
- Preserve trust assets
- Deal impartially with all beneficiaries
- Keep trust assets separate
- Enforce and defend any claims and actions against the trust
- Report and pay all state and federal taxes owed by the trust
- Comply with all terms of the trust
- Provide trust beneficiaries with complete and accurate information

WHO CAN BE YOUR TRUSTEE?

You, the grantor, can serve as the original trustee (or you and your spouse as co-trustees). Adult children may also serve as trustees or successor trustees. One child could serve alone or two or more could serve together as co-trustees.

Banks or trust companies may also be appointed to serve alone or as co-trustees with an individual that you name. Banks or trust companies are generally chosen by grantors who do not have the time, ability or desire to manage their own assets. There are a number of advantages to naming banks or trust companies. They are permanent. They don't die or move away. Such trustees are also financially accountable; you can always rest assured that state and federal examiners are watching the activities of banks and trust companies. In addition, banks and trust companies are impartial and experienced and provide professional investment management.

Individual trustees, on the other hand, serve under the honor system. There is no government agency looking over their shoulders to make sure that they are wise in the administration of your trust. People often choose individuals to serve as trustee because they may not charge a fee or you may wish to keep the trustees' fees in the family. In addition, individual trustees may have personal interest and knowledge of the beneficiaries and their special situations, or may have more specific investment or business expertise regarding unique trust assets. The selection of the trustee is vital to the viability of your estate plan. It merits careful thought and should not be taken lightly.

The same considerations regarding naming the trustee apply to naming your successor trustee. Who is best suited to serve as your successor trustee? Every situation is unique. There is no simple answer. You must weigh the pros and cons of naming an individual as your successor trustee or naming a bank or trust company.

Transfer the Following Assets Into Your Living Trust

- CDs
- Bank accounts
- Stocks and bonds
- Real estate
- Business assets
- Mutual funds

Funding Your Living Trust

It is not enough to create a living trust defining your objectives, naming your trustee and successor trustee and specifying how you would like your estate managed and distributed upon your death. You must transfer your assets from your sole name into your name as trustee of your trust. Once this is done, you no longer own your assets; the trust does. You do not lose control of your assets, however, because you control the trust and can revoke or change it at any time. The trust only controls assets that are titled in its name, so transferring should be done immediately.

Immediately after signing your trust, you, as grantor, will engage in this registration process. With your trust, your attorney will draft your will, which is often called a "pour-over will" because it directs that anything not in your trust be poured over into your trust at your death. Upon your death, any assets not registered in the name of your trust during your lifetime will be reregistered into the name of your trust by your executor, because your pour-over will pours all such assets over into your living trust to then be controlled by the successor trustee named in your living trust.

How to Reregister Assets Into the Name of Your Living Trust

The following is an example of titling assets into an individual living trust: "Jane Q. Public, Trustee of the Jane Q. Public Revocable Living Trust dated February 13, 2004." For married couples establishing a joint trust, the title would be "John Q. Public and Jane Q. Public, Trustees of the John Q. Public and Jane Q. Public Revocable Living Trust dated February 13, 2004."

During the process of transferring your assets into your living trust, someone may ask for the trust's tax identification number. You must use your own social security number for this purpose. The trust will not pay taxes or even file a tax return so long as you, the grantor, are trustee. You will pay taxes on the income earned by your trust on your personal 1040 federal income tax return and your state income tax return.

REAL ESTATE

A deed is required to retitle your real estate into the name of your living trust. Retitling real estate into your living trust raises four issues that must be considered:

1. **The realty transfer tax:** Many states require that a "recordation tax" or a "transfer tax" be paid upon the transfer of real property. There is often an exemption from this transfer tax for conveyances into a living trust. The exact language of the trust must be carefully reviewed to confirm that no transfer taxes would be due upon transferring your real estate into your trust.

2. **The due on sale clause on a mortgage secured by the real estate:** Due on sale clauses in existing mortgages must also be given careful consideration before recording a new deed. These types of provisions in mortgages protect the lender from the borrower transferring the real estate, still keeping it subject to the mortgage without first seeking the permission of the lender. If an unauthorized transfer of the real estate occurs, the due on sale clause in the mortgage may require the entire mortgage to be immediately paid in full. Mortgage lenders are not allowed to invoke the due on sale clause if the grantor of a living trust lives in his or her home and transfers the home in which he lives to a living trust. Therefore, on your personal residence, there is no concern with the due on sale clause in the mortgage document.

If the property being transferred into the trust is not occupied by the owner of the real estate, or if it is commercial real estate, the best practice is to notify the lender before transferring the real estate and obtain written assurances from the lender that the due on sale clause would not be enforced. Another reason to notify the mortgage lender before transferring real estate into a trust is that some lenders may require that the mortgage be rewritten, naming the trustee as the mortgagor.

---

3. **Notifying your homeowners or property and casualty insurance company to list your trust as a loss payee:** It is also important to notify the homeowners or property casualty insurance company when transferring real estate into a trust and have them issue a confirmation that the conveyance has not disturbed any insurance coverage.

4. Impact on owner's title insurance coverage should be considered: Because numerous title companies write owner's coverage, there are a number of different positions taken regarding the effect on owner's title coverage due to the conveyance of the real estate into a living trust. If continued owner's title insurance coverage in the real estate is important, contact the title company that wrote the owner's coverage and follow the procedures they recommend.

BANK ACCOUNTS

If you fund a living trust with your bank accounts, you must sign a new signature card for your accounts. You will register the assets into the name of your trust. Generally, a customer account representative at your bank can help you make this change. Some banks may require that you close an existing account and open a new one. If you do open a new account, be sure not to close the old one right away. Remember, closing out an account will affect any direct deposits received by that account. Change any direct deposits to go into the new account and wait until the new account receives at least one deposit before closing out the old account.

BANK CDs

Banks charge a penalty for early withdrawal of a certificate of deposit (CD). This may also apply to changing the registration of your CD into a living trust. Some banks, however, will waive the penalty if the transfer is going into a living trust. Since the trust maintains the same tax ID number (your social security number), there is no change in the taxable entity, only the title on the CD. If your bank will not waive the penalty, you must decide whether it would be better for you to transfer the CDs now and pay the penalty or wait and transfer the CDs into your trust after they mature.

STOCKS, BONDS AND MUTUAL FUNDS

To transfer stocks, bonds or mutual funds that you hold in a brokerage account into your trust, you need only reregister the name of the account to your trust. This is done by changing the registration of the account from your name alone into your name as trustee of your trust. Your broker or financial advisor can assist you with this. Brokerage accounts are the easiest vehicles to transfer because by simply reregistering the name on a brokerage account, you can move all of your investments in the account into your living trust.

If you own stocks or bonds in your name and hold the certificates, you will have to deal directly with the corporation or the borrower. Simply call the phone number that appears with the information you receive with your dividends. Tell the transfer agent that you wish to have them mail you the documents necessary to reregister your investments into another name. Although this is a simple process, every corporation has its own unique paperwork.

LIFE INSURANCE

Change the beneficiary of your life insurance to your trust by securing a change of beneficiary form from your life insurance agent.

IRAS AND QUALIFIED RETIREMENT PLANS

It may not be in your best interest to name your living trust the beneficiary of any IRAs or qualified retirement plans you own. Such a decision could cause unwanted tax consequences. Before acting, you should discuss these beneficiary designations with your attorney, CPA or your plan administrator to determine the alternatives available to you and the potential tax consequences. This consultation should be done before making any changes to these plans. The reason for the possible unwanted tax consequence is that IRAs and most qualified retirement plans permit the surviving spouse to roll over the deceased spouse's IRA or qualified retirement plan into her own plan. In other words, if a husband names his wife the beneficiary of his IRA, at the husband's death, his wife simply takes ownership of the IRAs and continues the income tax deferral. If someone other than his wife were to be beneficiary of such tax-deferred investments, there may be different income tax results.

The Operation of the Revocable Living Trust

Once you have completed the registration process, your living trust is now prepared to provide maximum benefits. Since the trust owns the assets registered in its name, the trust document offers a CONTINUUM OF CONTROL by clearly stating what happens to your assets no matter what happens to you. You keep complete control over all trust assets while you are healthy. You have named your successor trustee to step in and administer the assets of the trust in case you become incapacitated. Once you regain your capacity, your successor trustee will step down, and you will once again resume control as trustee. The successor trustee will only administer the trust while you are incapacitated. You may want to consider consulting your estate planning advisor about specific trusts designed with features for conservatorship.

In the event of your death, the executor you named in your will is instructed to pour over your assets into your trust. Debts will be paid and assets will be distributed by your successor trustee as you have specified in the trust document. Sometimes the pour-over will instructs that debts and expenses are to be paid from the probate estate prior to distribution to the trust. The trust identifies all beneficiaries to receive the assets upon your death, which would include family, charity and friends.

Tax Treatment of Revocable Living Trusts

A living trust is known as a GRANTOR TRUST because the trust's tax ID number is the same as the grantor's social security number. As a result, all tax events of the trust are reported on the grantor's personal income tax return. Therefore, so long as the grantor is serving as the trustee, the IRS does not require a separate tax return for the trust. When a bank or trust company serves as trustee, a separate tax ID number is required.

> As a grantor trust, there are no income tax advantages unique to a revocable living trust. There are certain inheritance and estate tax benefits that can be written into the living trust, but these same provisions could be written into a will and are, therefore, not unique to living trusts.

Disadvantages of Living Trusts

Despite all of the discussion and articles concerning the benefits of living trusts, they do have a number of disadvantages.

1. A LIVING TRUST IS MORE EXPENSIVE THAN A WILL TO ESTABLISH

The legal fees for a husband and wife for a living trust-centered estate plan can be significantly higher than the fee for a will. This higher expense may be justified by greater benefits. Even with a living trust, a will is still necessary to provide the pour-over benefits to sweep into the living trust assets that were not registered in the name of the trust during the grantor's life.

2. Living Trusts Are More Complex

The living trust must be "funded" by reregistering titles and beneficiary designations of all your investments to bring them under the control of the trust. Some women find this activity to be burdensome and not worth the effort. Living trusts can be amended by simply adding one- or two-page amendments to the existing trust. If one has a completely new living trust prepared, it might require going through the entire registration process again.

3. A Focus on Probate Avoidance Ignores Other Issues

Many people believe that simply having a living trust completes their estate planning. A fixation on probate avoidance can cause one to ignore deeper tax planning or family issues in the estate plan. Avoiding probate is not the most important aspect of your estate planning — using foresight to accomplish your own purposes is.

4. A Loss of Statutory Deadline for Creditors' Claims

One advantage of the probate process is that creditors must file claims against the estate of a deceased person within one year of the publication of the notice that the decedent has died. If one has her entire estate titled in the name of a living trust, and no one publishes the fact that the grantor has died, there is no statutory cutoff regarding the time that a creditor may have to bring a claim against the grantor's estate. The result is that a creditor could potentially bring a claim against the estate many years after death and attempt to collect the debt from the trust beneficiaries.

In order to cut off the claims of creditors against the estate of a decedent, many attorneys will still probate the pour-over will and publish the fact that a grantor is deceased. Some states, however, may have laws that do subject creditors of a trust to a limited time to collect. Most importantly, unless appropriate provisions are included in your trust and allowed by law, the living trust does not give protection from the claims of creditors during lifetime.

Considerations Regarding Divorce

Your estate plan, including your will and living trust, should be tailored to your current living situation. Divorce is one event that should initiate a woman to make a new will, change her living trust or review her beneficiaries. In some states, divorce changes by law some things regarding your property, but not necessarily all things. For example, you may reside in a state that does not change your life insurance, IRA or 401(k) beneficiaries in the event of your divorce. More often than not, you must do that specifically with each asset after you are divorced.

If you are considering a divorce, you ought to seriously consider the dramatic costs of divorce. It is never a win-win situation and can certainly take its toll on you and your estate. You should review your estate plan, as the process of divorce can take time. The law considers you legally married until the final divorce decree is signed by the judge. If you die during the divorce and do not have a will, your spouse will be entitled to the control and benefit of your estate. You ought to consider executing a will naming who you choose to be your beneficiaries and who will handle the distribution of your estate as your executor or personal representative.

Every state has rules regarding the obligation of spouses to care for each other in the event of death of one of them. Often this includes a share of money from the estate of the deceased spouse, often called a "spousal share" or "elective share," even if the one who died chose to cut her spouse out of her will. This is often dependent upon the length of your marriage and the children you have. Although you are still considered legally married if you die before the divorce is final, and your spouse is still entitled by law to elect to take a spousal share of your estate against your will, your will can help make your intent clear as to the distribution of your assets.

If you already have a will or a trust, you most likely have named your spouse as the executor and beneficiary. Review these documents and make changes as you deem necessary. Again, seek the advice of an attorney to find out the implications of the spousal election to which your estranged husband is still entitled to make against your will.

The beneficiaries on your life insurance, annuities, IRAs and retirement accounts should be reviewed. Federal law requires you to name your spouse as beneficiary on your company pensions, profit sharing and 401(k) plans. Your husband will need to agree in writing on a form provided by your employer to change it before you are divorced.

Update your medical directives and durable powers of attorney according to your best interests in light of the separation. Consider recording any revocations of prior documents. If you are named as a beneficiary on your parents' estate, discuss the aspect of placing your share in a trust to protect it from reach of the divorce.

You may also be entitled to a portion of your spouse's pension plan through his employer. A QDRO (Qualified Domestic Relations Order) is a court order required to divide a company pension plan which you will need to have your lawyer arrange and attach to your divorce decree as part of the property settlement of your divorce.

Once your divorce becomes final, update all your estate planning documents to take control of the distribution of your assets in the event of your death and the decision making in the event of your incapacity. As always, get good legal advice before making any changes and decisions. There are several steps to be taken:

1. **Update your will and other documents.** Execute a new will, changing your executor (if it was your former spouse) and renaming your beneficiaries. Any assets you and your husband held jointly were likely divided and retitled. Maintain

a certified copy of your divorce and keep it with your estate planning documents.

2. **Review beneficiaries on your nonprobate assets.** Consider any changes needed to life insurance policies, trusts, retirement plans, pension plans, annuities and any other asset that has a designated beneficiary.

3. **Update your powers of attorney and healthcare proxy.** Choose a new agent, if necessary, and be sure that your attorney, doctor, parent or someone you trust has a copy in the event of your incapacity.

Special Considerations in Remarriage or Single Parenting

All of these same updates and changes will apply in the circumstances of remarriage. Of particular consideration will also be how to plan for children from a previous marriage if your remarriage involves a blended family.

Couples need to seriously think through how to protect their new spouses, while also protecting their children. These areas need to be thoroughly discussed with your estate planning team. Open communication between you and your new spouse is always recommended.

If you die with children, the law presumes that the minor children will be adequately cared for by their other living natural parent, and not necessarily by whom those children live with or are being cared for. If you feel that the biological father of your children is not the best choice for your children's custody and care, indicate why in your will in a clearly factual manner and name your choice for custodian. There is no guarantee that a court will overcome the natural parent presumption, but courts are required to do what is in the best interests of the children, and your will may have an important bearing on that matter.

"What will happen to my children?"

When the doctors told Lydia she was dying of pancreatic cancer, her first concern was for her two preschool age children. Being a single parent, Lydia was their sole provider. The children had not seen their father in years as he had been in and out of incarceration. Lydia wanted to be sure to provide for their care and their best interests in the event of her death. She contacted an attorney to draft her will that named a custodian whom she thought would act in the best interests of her children, and she described the facts surrounding why the children's father was not now caring for them. She had peace of mind when she left the attorney's office knowing that a judge would now understand the complications of their family and act in the best interests of the children.

Special Considerations in the Death of Your Spouse

The death of a spouse is another event that may cause a woman to reconsider her estate plan. Remember that most women outlive their spouses by an average of seven years. The loss of a spouse is a very traumatic event and can cause great emotional turmoil and stress. The best time to plan for it is before it happens. The last thing you and your loved ones want to be doing is running around locating and updating documents or worrying about financial matters at your time of greatest grief. This is another important reason for women to take control of their finances and be informed.

What you are doing right now in reading and applying the steps in this guide is already alleviating that stress. For women, the failure to plan exacts a high price because it is most often women who must cope when loved ones become disabled or die. If you do find that you are suddenly a widow, consider taking the following measures, if necessary:

1. Change beneficiaries on life insurance and retirement plans.

2. Make sure assets have been transferred properly to fund trusts.

3. Review your estate distribution plan and update if necessary.

4. Update personal representatives, trustees, and guardians.

5. Review life insurance needs to ensure appropriate coverage, particularly if you have minor children.

Settling a Trust Estate

It is always a traumatic event whenever a loved one dies. The death of a spouse is particularly traumatizing. To be saddled with thinking about settling that loved one's estate can compound that trauma. A trust, however, makes that work all the more simple. Settling a trust estate is not difficult at all and can take a very short time if the trust was well planned and organized.

If you are called upon as a trustee to settle an estate, it may be helpful to follow these steps and guidelines in fulfilling your role as trustee. If the trust was a joint trust between you and your husband, you will likely continue using the trust even after his death. If the trust must be settled, however, there are just a few steps to take to do so. After important family members and friends have been notified and funeral arrangements have been made, the following is a list of steps to take:

1. Order certified copies of death certificates for each asset that will be transferred;

2. Check safety deposit boxes to inventory contents;

3. Make an appointment with your estate planning advisor;

4. Review trust instructions;

5. Notify life insurance and investment companies;

6. Be sure that all assets are moved into the trust;

7. Review business agreements, credit cards, size of the estate, allocation and distribution of assets;

8. File appropriate tax returns, including a final income tax return for the decedent; and

9. Distribute assets and personal effects.

Summary

The living trust is a versatile and beneficial estate planning document that should be considered by most women establishing their estate plans. In particular, the living trust should be considered by women who:

• Own real estate outside their home states;

• Own multiple properties;

• Have estates over $1,500,000 requiring federal estate tax planning;

• Feel that there is a potential for family conflict within their families after their death; or,

• Desire to benefit from one of the eight primary benefits of living trusts covered in this chapter.

As you can see, probate avoidance is not the only reason to give the living trust serious consideration. Avoiding the costs and hassles of probate is only one of many benefits that this estate planning tool can provide. Every woman should consider it in light of the type of life she leads and the advice she receives from her lawyer.

And now that you have taken the important step to understand trusts, the next step is to learn how to incorporate your retirement plan into your estate plan.

Step 6

Understand and Use Your Retirement Plan, 401(k)s and IRAs in Your Estate Plan

Topics Include

The Basic Types of Retirement Plans

Taxes That Affect Retirement Plans and IRAs

Retirement Plan Distributions During Lifetime and After Death

Naming Retirement Plan Beneficiaries

Introduction

*W*hile many women assume financial chores such as bill paying, household management and saving, they may have left the retirement planning to their husbands. Marriage has many wonderful benefits, but counting on your marriage for your retirement shouldn't be one of them. If you are single, you are already quite aware of that fact.

Taking into consideration community property laws or separate property laws with equitable distribution is important, particularly in the event of relocation, divorce or remarriage, and are worth discussing with your attorney. These may affect your estate, your estate plan and your retirement in the event of a divorce or remarriage. Whether you are a married woman or not, personal finance and retirement planning should be an integral part of your estate plan. In fact, according to the National Center for Women and Retirement Research, 95% of all women will have sole responsibility for their finances, yet 79% of all women have not planned for retirement.

Women may face unique challenges in the area of retirement planning due to many factors. Women generally have lower earnings and a higher job turnover due to family priorities. Women live longer and, therefore, need their retirement assets to last longer. Other factors such as child bearing, taking jobs without pension benefits to keep family priorities and being caregivers to loved ones also affect retirement funds. Married women usually outlive their husbands and often must provide their own retirement income after being widowed. If you can understand all of these challenges and start saving for retirement early on as part of your estate plan, the benefits will be beyond compare.

Like many women, your qualified retirement plan or individual retirement account may be your largest investment. It is ironic that the main cause for the growth in these plans — income tax deferral — is also the main cause of confusion concerning estate planning for qualified retirement plans and IRAs. The rules and regulations relating to retirement plans are complex. The EMPLOYEE RETIREMENT INCOME SECURITY ACT OF 1974 (ERISA) is the federal law covering pensions and other retirement programs. In addition to retirement plans governed by ERISA, there are traditional IRAs, Roth IRAs, 401(k) plans and 403(b) plans, among others.

In order to confirm the rules and regulations that govern your retirement plan, you must review your plan as well as your beneficiary designations. A comprehensive review should be undertaken at least annually, or more frequently, when there is a change in either the law or your financial status.

QUALIFIED RETIREMENT PLANS FOR EMPLOYEES

A qualified retirement plan is one in which the employer is entitled to an income tax deduction when contributions are made to the plan. This is permitted even if the employee is not required to include the amount as taxable income. The employer establishes the plan and determines the rights and opportunities of the participants, subject to IRS regulations.

A popular type of qualified retirement plan is the defined contribution plan. In this plan, the employer and/or employee contributes a specified amount throughout the year. The employer's contribution to the plan may or may not be fixed. The most familiar defined contribution plan is the 401(k) plan, where the participant elects to have a certain percentage of her compensation contributed to the plan. The amounts contributed to the plan are deferred from the participant's taxable federal income.

Many employers match a portion of the participant's contribution to the 401(k) plan. In several plans, the participants have some input into how contributions are allocated among investment options offered by the plan administrator.

Another type of qualified retirement plan is the 403(b) plan. These plans are specifically for employees of nonprofit organizations such as public schools, colleges and hospitals. These plans operate very much like 401(k) plans.

About 88% of women take some responsibility for their own investment accounts, annuities and life insurance according to a recent study by Prudential Financial Inc., though women may be more cautious in their investing. About half of the women polled plan to put more money away over the next year than they are doing now.

QUALIFIED RETIREMENT PLANS FOR INDIVIDUALS

Traditional IRAs

An IRA is essentially an individual's savings program with tax-deferred growth. The rules regarding IRAs are found in Internal Revenue Code §408, and it is easy to make generalizations about them. One must keep in mind, however, that what is true for an IRA is not necessarily the same for a qualified retirement plan; they are different in a number of ways. Most of the following discussion on IRAs concerns traditional IRAs.

Roth IRAs

The Taxpayer Relief Act of 1997 gave us a new type of IRA known as a ROTH IRA. There are a number of differences between the Roth IRA and the traditional IRA. One significant difference is that contributions to Roth IRAs are not income tax deductible. The benefit, however, is that distributions from Roth IRAs are generally not taxable as income.

Maximum IRA Contributions

- Contributions to a Roth IRA are not income tax deductible.

- The maximum contribution for Roth IRAs is the same as that for traditional IRAs:

  1. For 2004, it is $3,000.

  2. For 2005 through 2007, the maximum amount rises to $4,000.

  3. For 2008, the maximum contribution reaches $5,000.

  4. The amount one can contribute to a Roth IRA is phased out for single taxpayers beginning with income over $95,000, or $150,000 for married taxpayers.

Income Tax-Free Withdrawals From Roth IRAs

Roth IRA contributions can be withdrawn at any time without any restrictions, taxes or penalties. Distributions of earnings from Roth IRAs are not included in income under certain situations:

- You must be at least 59½ years old, and

- You must have held the account for a minimum of five years. (There are exceptions to this rule based on death, disability or for first-time homebuyers.)

- There is no requirement to start withdrawing money when you reach age 70½. In fact, you can continue to make contributions after that age. (This is the most significant difference between Roth IRAs and traditional IRAs.)

Due to the unique features of the Roth IRA, the rest of the discussions of this chapter will be referring only to the traditional IRA and not the Roth IRA.

Taxes Affecting Qualified Retirement Plans and IRAs

Taxes must be carefully considered when making decisions about lifetime distributions from retirement plans or choosing retirement plan beneficiaries. The following are some tax traps of which to be aware:

10% Penalty Tax on Plan Distributions Taken Too Soon

When distributions are received from retirement plans or traditional IRAs before the participant is 59½ years old, there is a 10% penalty on the amount received. In addition to the penalty, income tax is due on the amount withdrawn from the retirement plan.

The 10% penalty does not apply if the distribution is made because of the death or total disability of the participant or to make medical payments on his or her behalf. It also does not apply for qualified education expenses or for limited amounts used for a first-time home purchase. In addition, the penalty does not apply if the amount withdrawn is rolled over into another IRA or qualified retirement plan within 60 days of taking the distribution. There is also an exemption from the 10% penalty for substantially equal periodic payments. This is a withdrawal system in which the IRA is depleted by taking substantially equal payments over the lifetime of the participant and a designated beneficiary.

PENALTY-FREE WITHDRAWALS

Penalty-free withdrawals are permitted from qualified retirement plans and IRAs as follows:

- Attain age 59½

- Death

- Disability

- Certain medical expenses

- Higher education expenses (IRA only)

- Health insurance premiums while unemployed (IRA only)

- Up to $10,000 for first-time home buyers (IRA only)

50% PENALTY TAX ON PLAN DISTRIBUTIONS NOT TAKEN SOON ENOUGH

All qualified retirement plans and traditional IRAs require the participant to begin receiving distributions from the plan no later than her required beginning date (RBD). The required beginning date is April 1 of the calendar year following the year in which the participant reaches age 70½.

The IRS has tables that establish life expectancy factors to be used by participants to determine the minimum distribution required to be received from the retirement plan or IRA. If the minimum distribution is not received, a penalty of 50% is imposed on the difference between the actual distribution received and the minimum distribution required.

INCOME TAX (INCOME IN RESPECT OF A DECEDENT)

After the participant's death, if a beneficiary receives a distribution from the retirement plan or IRA, the distribution is taxable income to the beneficiary (at the beneficiary's tax rate) as income in respect of a decedent. If the proceeds are payable to the participant's estate, the entire amount is taxed at the estate's income tax rate. If the distribution is payable to the participant's surviving spouse, she may elect to roll over the distribution into a new IRA, thereby avoiding tax due to income in respect of decedent and continuing to defer the income tax.

This rule is based on the fact that during the participant's lifetime, the assets in the retirement plan were not taxed. Therefore, after death, whoever inherits the retirement plan is required to pay the income tax. For this reason, retirement plans are only tax deferred, not tax exempt.

FEDERAL ESTATE TAX

For estates greater than the lifetime exemption amount ($1,500,000 in 2004), the value of retirement plans and IRAs owned by the participant are subject to the federal estate tax upon death. Generally, the full amount of the retirement plan is taxed in the participant's estate for federal estate tax purposes. If, however, the participant's surviving spouse is the beneficiary, it is possible that there will be no estate taxes due to the unlimited marital deduction.

Estate Planning for Retirement Plan Distributions During Lifetime

A key strategy regarding estate planning for retirement plan distributions is income tax deferral. If the participant can afford it, she should consider deferring distributions from her IRA or retirement plan as long as possible. This deferral will permit the continued growth of the plan on a tax-deferred basis. The law requires that certain minimum distributions be taken from the plan. The reason for this policy is that these plans have been established to be retirement plans and not wealth-building plans. These minimum distribution rules are intended to force funds out of the plan and expose the required distributions to income tax.

MINIMUM DISTRIBUTION RULES

Annual minimum distributions (known as "minimum required distributions" or MRDs) to the plan participant are required to begin on or before the participant's required beginning date (RBD). The RBD for IRAs is April 1 of the year following the calendar year in which the participant reaches age 70½. For 403(b) and 401(k) plans, the RBD is the later of April 1 of the year following the year in which the participant reaches age 70½ or retires. Once the participant has reached his required beginning date, the IRS rules establish the minimum annual distributions that must be taken by the plan participant. The MRD must be taken by December 31 of each year.

The minimum distribution required from your plan or traditional IRA is calculated in two steps:

Step One: Determine the total value of the investments in all your retirement plan accounts as of the last day of last year.

Step Two: Find your age as of the end of this year on the Uniform Table and divide the total value of your investments by the "applicable divisor" listed by your age.

Consider the case of Mrs. Johnson whose husband died last year. She is alone, owns her home and has enough income to live on. She will be 72 at the end of this year and has $100,000 in her only IRA, as valued at the end of last year. Based on her age and the value of her IRA, she must receive a minimum of $3,906.25 during this year to avoid the 50% penalty ($100,000 divided by 25.6). Since she is spending a lot of time alone, but is in good health, her friends have been bugging her to get away and travel to the Holy Lands, which she has always wanted to do. Mrs. Johnson decides to spend her required distributions on a Mediterranean cruise throughout the Middle East, instead of allowing the government to take half of this potential income in taxes.

The beneficiary of your IRA can be changed after your required beginning date without having any effect upon the required distribution amount. Also, the distribution amount is not based upon whom you name as the beneficiary of your account after your death. The minimum required distribution is calculated the same way whether you name a charity, a family member, an older parent or younger child as your beneficiary. The only exception to this rule is if you are (1) married to a person who is more than 10 years younger than you and (2) your spouse is the only beneficiary of your IRA. If that is your situation, the required distributions are based on the actual joint life expectancy of you and your younger spouse and are lower than the Uniform Table.

Uniform Table for Determining Applicable Divisor			
Age	**Applicable Divisor**	**Age**	**Applicable Divisor**
70	27.4	93	9.6
71	26.5	94	9.1
72	25.6	95	8.6
73	24.7	96	8.1
74	23.8	97	7.6
75	22.9	98	7.1
76	22.0	99	6.7
77	21.2	100	6.3
78	20.3	101	5.9
79	19.5	102	5.5
80	18.7	103	5.2
81	17.9	104	4.9
82	17.1	105	4.5
83	16.3	106	4.2
84	15.5	107	3.9
85	14.8	108	3.7
86	14.1	109	3.4
87	13.4	110	3.1
88	12.7	111	2.9
89	12.0	112	2.6
90	11.4	113	2.4
91	10.8	114	2.1
92	10.2	115 +	1.9

Remember: This table is unisex. Compared to actual life expectancies, this tends to create unique issues for women because they live longer than men but are forced to take taxable distributions based on the shorter time period (both in expectancy and distribution periods). Again, this is all the more reason for women to plan smart.

DESIGNATED BENEFICIARIES

The designated beneficiary of a retirement plan or IRA must be an individual to achieve certain tax benefits. Since the participant's estate or charity is not an individual, the IRS does not consider either one to be a designated beneficiary. In addition to naming one individual, an acceptable beneficiary could be a group of individuals (for example, "all my children"). When a group of individuals is named, the life expectancy of the oldest member of the group is used to calculate the required minimum distribution. In addition, all members in the group must be individuals. (Under certain limited circumstances, a trust may be named a beneficiary and the trust beneficiaries will be treated as designated beneficiaries if every trust beneficiary is an individual.)

The designated beneficiary does not have to be finally determined until September 30 of the year following the year of the participant's death. This permits many planning opportunities. A person who was designated a beneficiary on the date of the participant's death, but is not a beneficiary as of September 30 (for reasons other than his death), is not considered a designated beneficiary. This provides ample room for post-death planning. Therefore, once a participant has died, it is important to engage the services of an experienced estate planner before making any distributions from her plan or IRA.

Because of the possibility of many decades of continued income tax deferral after the participant's death, it is a preferred strategy to name as the beneficiary of an IRA an individual who is younger than the participant. If there are concerns about the younger beneficiary not managing the assets correctly, you could have the IRA benefits payable to a trust for the benefit of your grandchildren, for example.

Married women need to understand and participate in the direction and control the marital investments take. It may be favorable to fund the wife's IRA first due to her longer life expectancy and the possibility of limited funds later. Similarly, a young couple has an interest in funding the wife's ROTH IRA first due to the advantage of tax-free earnings coupled with no minimum distributions (compared to traditional IRAs at 70½).

Spouse as Designated Beneficiary

If you are married, there are a number of significant benefits to naming your spouse the sole beneficiary of your retirement plan or IRA. One benefit is that (regardless of whether you die before or after your RBD), he has the option to roll over your IRA tax free into his own IRA. The benefit of a tax-free spousal rollover is that the surviving spouse can defer taking the MRDs until he is 70½. In addition, the spouse can name a beneficiary of the rollover IRA to achieve continued income tax deferral over another lifetime.

If your spouse does not roll over your IRA into his own, he must leave the benefits in your IRA and take required distributions over his life expectancy. If you die before age 70½, the payments can be deferred until the year you would have reached 70½. If your spouse is older than you, waiting until you would have reached age 70½ before taking the first distribution allows him to defer the commencement of distribution for as long as possible, allowing the longer tax-deferred growth of the IRA.

Another benefit to naming your spouse the beneficiary of your IRA is that if your spouse is more than 10 years younger than you, the distribution period will be longer and, therefore, the required minimum distributions will be less than would be required for a nonspouse beneficiary.

Consider the case of Jane Doe who is married and has named her husband, John, as the beneficiary of the IRA. John is more than 10 years younger than Jane. Jane will be 72 at the end of the year, but her husband is only 60. Jane has IRA holdings that amount to $100,000. If Jane was single, or John was less than 10 years younger, Jane's mandatory minimum distribution would be $3,906.25 ($100,00 divided by 25.6 — the applicable distribution period), but because John is more than 10 years younger, Jane uses a different IRS table. In Jane's case, her required distribution is $3,703.74 ($100,000 divided by 27 — the applicable distribution period).

A woman retiring at age 55 can, on the average, expect to live another 27 years or more. That's at least four years longer than a man retiring at the same age. Women need to plan and save for these extra years.

Are You Entitled to Benefits From Your Husband's Retirement Plan?

If you are a beneficiary under your husband's pension plan, you may request a copy of a summary plan description from the plan administrator (usually the employer) that describes the plan, your rights as a spouse under the plan and whether survivor annuities or other death benefits are provided under the plan. There may be a charge for this service, but it may prove to be worthwhile for you. You may also make a written request for copies of plan documents and a statement describing your spouse's vested benefits under the plan.

Social Security retirement benefits are important to be aware of, but will not likely be enough to live on in retirement. Women's Social Security benefits are generally lower than men's because of job changes and being out of work to care for family priorities. This fact makes retirement planning all the more significant.

Estate Planning for Retirement Plan Distributions After Death

In computing the required distributions to the beneficiaries of retirement plans after the death of the participant, the first consideration is the participant's age at the time of her death. If the participant dies before her RBD, then one set of rules applies. If the participant dies after her RBD, another set of rules applies.

IF PARTICIPANT DIES BEFORE THE REQUIRED BEGINNING DATE

If the participant dies before her RBD, a nonspouse beneficiary must take required distributions over his life expectancy. If there are multiple beneficiaries who are all individuals, the distributions must be taken over the life expectancy of the oldest individual.

If the participant dies before her RBD and there is no designated beneficiary, then benefits must be distributed to the nonindividual beneficiary no later than December 31 of the year that contains the fifth anniversary of the participant's death. This is known as the five-year rule.

IF PARTICIPANT DIES AFTER THE REQUIRED BEGINNING DATE

If a participant dies after her RBD, remaining plan benefits or IRAs must be paid to a designated beneficiary over a period of time, which is the longer of the beneficiary's life expectancy or the participant's life expectancy. If there are multiple beneficiaries and the plan is not divided into separate accounts, distributions must be made over the life expectancy of the oldest individual beneficiary.

For purposes of calculating the required minimum distribution, the designated beneficiary is determined on September 30 of the year following the year of the participant's death (the DETERMINATION DATE). Thus, there is time allowed to formulate a strategy to create the longest possible payout. This could be done using disclaimers, for example.

If there is no designated beneficiary as of the determination date, the distribution period is the remaining life expectancy of the participant.

When a woman is not the primary wage earner in the family, the tendency for that family may be to fully fund the husband's company 401(k), 403(b) or other retirement plan, with nothing accruing to the wife unless a QDRO is enforceable (which is only in the event of separation or divorce). Women need to think about how to avoid this predicament. At a minimum, in circumstances when the couple funds the husband's retirement plan for the family, the wife's IRAs should be funded for the family benefit as well to allow both marriage partners to have some form of long-term retirement assets available.

For both traditional and ROTH IRAs, a spouse without earned income can still fund (and deduct for traditional IRAs) those IRAs up to the limits allowed for the wage earner's income.

Estate Planning Considerations When Naming IRA and Retirement Plan Beneficiaries

CHARITY AS BENEFICIARY

If the participant dies before her RBD, the retirement plan or IRA will be treated as having no designated beneficiary and the five-year rule will apply. By specifying that the charitable organization is entitled to a separate account of the IRA, this result can be avoided. Therefore, when naming a charity as a beneficiary of a retirement plan or IRA, it is important to specify the specific portion or account that goes to the charity.

Many people with charitable intent have accumulated large IRAs. The amount given to charity can be enhanced by giving the portion of their estate made up of retirement plans or IRAs to charity. This amount will not be subject to income tax when distributed to the charity and, in addition, will be a deduction from the federal estate tax.

> Gwen had an estate made up of $50,000 cash and an IRA valued at $50,000, for a total of $100,000. She wanted to leave $50,000 to her college because she felt that her education had made her successful throughout her life. She wished to divide the remainder of her estate equally between her two children. Gwen went to her attorney and told him that she wanted to give the $50,000 in cash to her alma mater. This would allow her children to share the $50,000 IRA. Fortunately, she had a knowledgeable attorney who had a much better plan.
>
> Her attorney explained that if the cash went to the college and the IRA to the children, the children would have to pay income tax as they received the IRA distributions. On the other hand, if the college was named the beneficiary of the IRA, the college, a nonprofit educational organization (a charity), would receive the $50,000 from the IRA tax free.

CHARITABLE REMAINDER TRUST AS BENEFICIARY

An excellent option is to name a CHARITABLE REMAINDER TRUST the beneficiary of your IRA. You should consider this option if you wish to provide an income stream for your surviving spouse or aged parents, yet also make a charitable contribution. Please see Step 7 for a detailed discussion of charitable trusts.

You can create a charitable remainder trust during your lifetime and name the charitable trust the beneficiary of your IRA. Then, upon your death, your IRA or retirement plan is distributed to the charitable remainder trust since it is the designated beneficiary of your plan. The charitable trust will then make distributions to your surviving spouse (or whoever you named as the income beneficiary) for his life, and upon his death, the trust assets will be distributed to your named charity.

Upon the death of your surviving spouse, the charitable trust terminates and the assets remaining are paid to one or more of your favorite charities. If your surviving spouse is the only income beneficiary of the charitable trust, then the entire value of the IRA passing to the charitable remainder trust will be deductible for estate tax purposes upon your death. This is because your surviving spouse's interest qualifies for the marital deduction and the trust assets going to charity qualify for the charitable deduction. There is no federal income tax due when the IRA is paid to the trust upon your death because the charitable remainder trust is tax exempt. Your surviving spouse, however, must pay income tax on the amount that he receives from the trust each year.

A second strategy is to name your children the income beneficiaries of your charitable trust. The charitable remainder trust would be designated the contingent beneficiary of your retirement plan or IRA with your spouse being named the primary beneficiary. The result is that during lifetime, both you and your spouse have full lifetime rights to the plan assets. After the death of both you and your spouse, the undistributed assets in the retirement plan or IRA will pass to the charitable remainder trust in a lump sum and provide income to your children for their lifetimes. Since the charitable remainder trust pays no income tax, the transfer of your retirement plan benefits into the charitable remainder trust is tax free.

This plan benefits your children because they receive the income from the full value of your retirement plan or IRA assets since they are not reduced by income tax. In addition, your estate receives an estate tax charitable deduction for the present value of the remainder interest that will go to charity upon the death of your children. Your children may actually receive more from the charitable remainder trust during their lifetimes than they would have received from your qualified plan. In terms of wealth replacement, since the charitable remainder trust does not pay out to charity until the death of your children, the wealth replacement is not necessary until your children's death and not your death. The wealth replacement insurance will be less because of insuring a younger generation.

A third benefit of naming a charitable remainder trust the beneficiary of your retirement plans relates to the challenges when wanting to name a parent or other older nonspouse person the beneficiary of your retirement plan. Naming an older person squeezes the benefits out of your plan in a relatively short period of time because of the older person's short life expectancy. Income taxes get paid up front, and the elderly person will have less money available in his later years. If, on the other hand, the retirement plan benefits are left to a charitable remainder trust with an elderly income beneficiary, the elderly person will enjoy a steady stream of income from the charitable remainder trust that will last for her lifetime. In addition, your estate will get an estate tax charitable deduction.

TRUSTS FOR NONSPOUSE INDIVIDUALS AS BENEFICIARY

A trust is not an individual and, therefore, does not qualify for the *tax benefits* reserved for designated beneficiaries who are individuals. In limited circumstances, nevertheless, IRS regulations will allow a trust the same benefits reserved for individuals as designated beneficiaries. The concept is that the IRS will "look through" the trust and identify the individual beneficiaries of the trust as though they were individual beneficiaries of the IRA or retirement plan for purposes of calculating the minimum distribution amount. In order for a trust to qualify for such favorable treatment, it must satisfy four requirements:

1. The trust must be valid under state law.

2. The trust beneficiaries must be individuals identifiable from the trust document. (This is necessary because the age of the oldest beneficiary is used to calculate the required minimum distribution amount.)

3. The trust must be irrevocable or become so after the participant's death.

4. A copy of the trust documentation must be given to the plan administrator.

These requirements must be satisfied no later than December 31 of the year following the year in which the participant dies. The only exception to this rule is if the spouse is the sole designated beneficiary of the trust and the spouse is more than 10 years younger than the participant, then these requirements must be in place at the participant's RBD.

Even if there is only one trust beneficiary that is not an individual (for example, a charity), the entire trust will be treated as having no individual named as a designated beneficiary. As a result, trust assets will be required to be paid out over the life expectancy of the participant and not that of any individual beneficiaries of the trust. If the participant dies before her RBD and a trust has a nonindividual beneficiary, benefits must be distributed no later than December 31 of the year that contains the fifth anniversary of the participant's death.

This negative result may be eliminated by having "nonindividual" beneficiaries cash out or disclaim their interest in the trust or placing their interest into separate accounts before September 30 of the year following the year of the participant's death.

In addition, the trust must state that it is not to use any IRA distributions to pay debts or expenses of the participant's estate, including federal and state taxes. Without such language in the trust, the participant may be treated as not having a designated beneficiary since the participant's estate will be treated as a beneficiary of the retirement plan or IRA.

Q-TIP TRUST FOR SPOUSE AS BENEFICIARY

Many IRA and qualified retirement plan participants desire to provide for their surviving spouses for life, continue the income tax deferral on their plans for as long as possible and at the same time maintain control over the ultimate disposition of the remaining benefits at the death of their surviving spouses. In addition, they may desire to qualify their retirement plans for the unlimited marital deduction from the federal estate tax. To achieve these multiple goals, the participant must name a trust the beneficiary of her plan or IRA.

> Only the Q-TIP trust qualifies for the marital deduction from estate tax at the participant's death and, at the same time enables the participant to control her trust assets after the death of her surviving spouse.

If the participant dies before age 70½ and her surviving spouse is the sole designated beneficiary of her plan or IRA, payments do not have to begin to be made to the surviving spouse until the participant would have reached age 70½. If a Q-TIP trust is used, however, the ultimate beneficiaries of the Q-TIP trust are treated as the designated beneficiaries of the plan or IRA, and the rule permitting the surviving spouse to postpone distributions until the participant would have reached age 70½ is not available. The result is that distributions from the plan or IRA must begin in the year immediately following the year of the participant's death.

A woman can save toward retirement even if she doesn't belong to an employer-sponsored pension plan. Anyone receiving compensation, or married to someone receiving compensation, may contribute to an IRA.

A woman who is self employed can start a Keogh plan, a Simplified Employment Plan (SEP) or a Savings Incentive Match Plan for Employees of Small Employers (SIMPLE).

CREDIT SHELTER TRUST FOR SPOUSE AS BENEFICIARY

It may not be advisable to name a credit shelter trust the beneficiary of your retirement plan or IRA. One disadvantage is that naming the trust the beneficiary (instead of your spouse) prevents your surviving spouse from rolling over the funds into his own IRA. Another disadvantage to using IRAs to fund the credit shelter trust is that the IRA's distributions may be subject to income tax when received by the trust, and the trust's income tax rate might be higher than the surviving spouse's. In addition, if the trust pays the taxes, it reduces the amount that will pass free of federal estate tax from the credit shelter trust upon the death of the surviving spouse. There are cases, however, when a substantial portion of a participant's estate is made up of plan benefits and IRAs and there are no other assets available to fund the credit shelter trust.

There are two basic strategies to using retirement plans or IRAs to fund the credit shelter trust of the first spouse to die:

1. First, the participant could designate the credit shelter trust the beneficiary of the participant's IRAs only to the extent necessary to fund the credit shelter trust.

2. A second option is to name the spouse the primary beneficiary and the credit shelter trust the contingent beneficiary.

Using the second approach, if the participant dies before her spouse, the surviving spouse has the option to disclaim the exact value of IRAs needed to fully fund the participant's credit shelter trust. The remaining portion of the IRA not disclaimed could be rolled over into the surviving spouse's IRA. This option is preferred due to its flexibility. If the estate tax is repealed, or if the participant has other available assets, the surviving spouse can simply roll over the deceased spouse's IRA into his own IRA. (Retaining and rolling over retirement funds whenever possible is always a good idea, as this avoids heavy taxes.) In addition, the use of the disclaimer strategy enables the surviving spouse to compare the benefit of tax-deferred income with the benefit of estate tax savings at the time of the participant's death. To maintain the option to disclaim, the designation of the spouse should remain revocable during the life of the participant.

Caution When Naming Trust for Spouse as Beneficiary

As mentioned in this chapter, there are several estate planning reasons why you may want to name a trust for your spouse as beneficiary of your retirement plan or IRA. Such a trust could save estate taxes, protect children from a prior marriage and also protect the benefits from your spouse's financial inexperience or creditors. The price to be paid, however, is that the trust benefits generally must begin to be paid the year after your death and the IRA loses the many benefits of the tax-free spousal rollover IRA when a trust is used.

Summary

Many people forget to consider retirement plans and IRAs when doing estate planning. Women particularly need to give this area of planning meticulous thought due to longer life expectancies and tendencies to not look toward retirement early enough in life.

The importance of coordinating the beneficiary designation on your retirement plans and IRAs with your estate plan cannot be overstated. Whether single or married, women must see their own retirement planning as part of their overall estate plan.

As this chapter demonstrates, it is important to discuss these concepts and strategies with your estate planning team to help assess your situation and goals. Together, your team can work with you to develop a long-term plan that will accomplish your goals and dreams. In addition, with the number of taxes involved with retirement plan benefits, distribution during both lifetime and after death should be carefully considered.

Step 7

Make the World a Better Place With Charitable Estate Planning

Introduction

ACCORDING TO "GIVING USA: THE ANNUAL REPORT ON PHILANTHROPY," Americans gave $241 billion to charities in 2003. And many of those gifts were motivated by women. Lifetime gifts by individuals totaled approximately $179 billion, and gifts by wills represented about $22 billion. That means that 75% of philanthropy came from individuals, a remarkable testament to the generosity of Americans. This chapter covers some of the basic rules and plans available to you.

Women are notable givers and are fast becoming notable wage earners. According to "A Woman's Guide to Investing," statistics gathered by OppenheimerFunds, Lightbulb Press and MassMutual Financial Group demonstrate that American women earn over $2.1 trillion annually. Over 40% of affluent Americans are women. Women in the United States own 46% of privately held businesses. Women control their financial destiny and do a lot of philanthropy in the process.

Some researchers predict that over the next 35 years, as much as $41 trillion will be transferred from the parents of baby boomers to their children. Charitable giving will play an immense role in this transfer of wealth. Although charitable estate planning provides many personal and tax benefits, it has a more fundamental benefit in that it puts the control of how to help society in the hands of the donor. With proper planning, individuals can direct money that would have been taken from them in the form of income taxes, capital gains taxes or gift and estate taxes to a charitable cause that has special meaning to them. This chapter provides a broad framework within which to consider charitable gifts.

What Is Charitable Estate Planning?

The motivations for making charitable gifts are as numerous as the women making them. Gifts are given to hospitals, cancer funds and heart associations in memory of loved ones who have died from health challenges. Gifts are also given to colleges and universities with a view toward helping the disadvantaged receive the quality education that the donor received. Gifts are given by women to benefit men, women and children's concerns around the world. Whether the motivation is based on religious conviction, a long-term relationship with a charity or a desire to leverage the tax benefits, charitable estate planning is full of opportunities and emerging possibilities to increase and maximize gift assets, save taxes and provide for heirs all at the same time. In addition, many families are beginning to realize that transferring the values of the senior generation to the younger generation is equally as important as getting a tax benefit. Using charitable estate planning to transfer both your values and your assets to the next generation is a true legacy.

WHAT IS A CHARITABLE GIFT?

In general, a gift that qualifies for favorable tax treatment must meet three tests. First, the donor must give up all control of the gift and, with a few exceptions, there can be no strings attached to the gift. Second, the donor must deliver the gift to a qualified charity. Lastly, if the donor receives a benefit from the gift above a nominal amount, the donor can claim as a deduction only the net contribution after taking into account a benefit received.

WHAT IS A QUALIFIED CHARITY?

When donors make charitable contributions, the amount they can claim as a deduction for income tax purposes depends on the type of qualified charity. A qualified charity is one that is a charitable organization as described in Internal Revenue Code §501(c)(3). Such organizations will be referred to throughout this chapter as charities. All nonprofit organizations are defined by the IRS as either "public charities" or "private foundations." Public charities are churches, schools, hospitals and medical research organizations, for example. All public charities rely on public support. Private foundations, on the other hand, are usually funded by an individual or corporation and receive no support from the public. As discussed later, the annual charitable contribution ceilings differ for gifts to public charities as opposed to private foundations. All qualified charities have a tax-exempt status letter from the IRS and would be happy to send a copy to a potential donor upon request.

Income Tax Benefits of Charitable Gifts

In general, donors who itemize deductions on their federal income tax return may claim a charitable contribution income tax deduction up to certain limits each year. The income tax deduction limits are based on the type of organization that the donor is contributing to as well as the type of assets that make up the gift. For gifts of cash to public charities, the donor may claim a deduction of up to 50% of the donor's adjusted gross income. There is a five-year carry-forward period to claim any excess above the 50% ceiling. For gifts of appreciated capital assets held more than 12 months, the contribution ceiling is 30% of adjusted gross income with the same five-year carry-forward period to use up the excess.

The contribution ceilings are slightly different for gifts to private foundations. Cash contributions are limited to 30% of the donor's adjusted gross income. Gifts of long-term appreciated assets (owned by the donor for 12 months and a day) are limited to 20% of adjusted gross income. In all cases, the same five-year carry-forward period applies. None of these limits apply to charitable gifts made from an estate.

It is important to note that these percentage limits are for income tax deductions only. There are no contribution ceilings for gifts made at death.

ADDITIONAL BENEFITS FROM CONTRIBUTING APPRECIATED ASSETS

Individuals often own appreciated assets such as stock, real estate or art objects. In general, as long as the asset has been owned by the same donor for 12 months and a day, the donor can claim the fair market value of the assets as a charitable contribution tax deduction.

This benefits the donor in two ways. First, the donor completely avoids the capital gains tax that would have resulted from a sale by the donor, and second, the donor benefits from a tax saving from a deduction on the full fair market value of the asset. For noncash assets valued over $5,000, the donor must get an independent qualified appraisal in order to substantiate her charitable deduction. The IRS prescribes guidelines for the appraisals, and most charities can assist the donor with the correct reporting forms and rules.

It is also important to note that for gifts of tangible personal property (art, cars, antiques), the donor can claim the full fair market value as a tax deduction only if the charity can use the item in a manner related to its exempt purpose. Otherwise, the deduction is the lesser of the fair market value or the cost basis.

GIFTS UNIQUE TO REAL ESTATE

- Gifts of a Remainder Interest in a Home or Farm

Normally, in order for a gift to be deductible for income tax purposes, the donor must donate to charity all of her rights to the assets. One exception to this rule is the transfer to a charity of a personal residence or farm, but reserving a life estate. The donor conveys by deed her home, vacation property or farm to the charity while reserving the right to continue using the property until death.

In exchange for this transfer, the donor is entitled to an income tax deduction on the present value of the ultimate gift to the charity. The gift of the remainder interest in a home need not be the entire interest but could be a portion of the acreage — for example, only two acres out of a 10-acre tract of land, if that is what consists of the donor's home. The gift of the remainder interest for a farm also need not be the entire farm acreage but may be any portion of the total acreage used as a farm. Saving the family home or farm is often an important consideration for many women.

Generally, the donor agrees to pay the insurance, maintenance and other expenses on the property. At death, the charity is able to sell the property and use the proceeds for its charitable purposes. Such a gift could work well for both the donor and the charity when the donor's property is contiguous to the charity's headquarters.

– The Gift of an Undivided Portion of a Donor's Interest in Real Estate

Transferring to charity only a portion of the donor's total interest in real estate qualifies as a gift that is deductible for income tax purposes. The gift of a partial interest in real estate commonly occurs when the donor is planning to sell highly appreciated real estate. For example, a donor may give a charity an undivided one-third interest as tenant in common in a farm or commercial property. The donor receives an immediate income tax deduction based upon the value of the one-third interest. When the real estate is eventually sold, the donor receives two-thirds of the sales proceeds and the charity receives the other one-third. With this strategy, the donor receives a charitable deduction for a portion of the property's total value and avoids the capital gains tax on the gift portion, too.

A gift of an undivided interest is also possible with a piece of artwork whereby the charity receives, for example, an undivided 50% interest and is allowed to exhibit the work for six months out of the year. Often, donors give an undivided interest in an asset to charity because they cannot claim a deduction for the entire asset in one year or because they also want to enjoy the asset for part of the time.

– Conservation Easements

Conservation easements enable the donor to receive an income tax deduction for preserving her land in its existing state. The most significant benefit to the landowner, however, may not be tax related. The landowner will have the peace of mind that her land will remain as she has left it.

A conservation easement places restrictions on the use and future development of land. The terms of the easement are written in an easement agreement that is recorded in the recorder of deeds office in the county in which the land is located. The easement describes the limits placed on the use of the land by the current and any future landowner. The easement is a perpetual restriction on the use of the land.

The restrictions that qualify as conservation easements include using land only for outdoor recreation or for preserving open space as forest or farmland pursuant to a government conservation policy. Historically important land areas and certified historic structures also qualify. The conservation easement must be granted to a qualified organization such as a local government or a publicly supported charity.

The donor receives a charitable deduction based upon the value of the development rights that the donor gave up in the conservation easement. These values must be determined by a qualified appraiser. There are no specified limits on use that are required for all conservation easements. One donor may choose to restrict all possible commercial development on her farm, while her neighbor might permit limited subdivision. The more subdivision or development that the donor permits, the lower the value of the easement, which results in a lower income tax deduction.

The organizations qualified to receive conservation easements are either government bodies or public charities known as land trusts. Officials of the land trust (or the government agency) will inspect the property periodically over the years to confirm that it is being used in compliance with the terms of the conservation easement.

The value of the conservation easement permitted as a federal income tax deduction is limited to 30% of the donor's contribution base. Any income tax deduction not taken in the year of the gift can be carried forward for an additional five years. The value of the land with the easement will be much lower for purposes of the federal estate tax.

CHARITABLE ESTATE PLANNING WITH IRAS AND QUALIFIED RETIREMENT PLANS

If a donor wishes to leave a bequest to a charity, the donor would be advised to look first to an IRA or another qualified retirement plan. In general, a retirement plan has the potential of being decimated by taxes at death by both the income tax and the estate tax. It is possible that a donor could lose over 50% of the plan's value to taxes at death. On the other hand, if the donor names a charity as the beneficiary of a retirement plan, there is zero tax at death … no income tax and no estate tax. Please see Step 6 for detailed strategies on using your IRA and retirement plan for giving to charities.

Charitable Giving Can Be the Foundation of a Good Estate Plan

Tiffany wanted to know how much tax she would have to pay when her estate was settled. An initial analysis revealed that because she had several IRAs and she was leaving those proceeds to a niece and nephew, the tax rate was over 45%! She had a heart for missions and always tithed generously. By restructuring her estate plan and leaving her IRAs to missions and other assets to her niece and nephew, she reduced the taxes from 45% on the IRAs to zero, and the cost of leaving a gift to her niece and nephew from her other assets was only 15%.

Charitable Giving Strategies

OUTRIGHT GIFTS TO CHARITIES

While there are a wide variety of gift methods that provide a range of tax benefits, income payments or other advantages to the donor, the simplest form of philanthropy is the straight, outright gift. Such gifts benefit the charity immediately and afford the donor the largest possible charitable deduction. Direct gifts can be made in the form of cash, securities, mutual funds, personal property, life insurance or real estate.

BARGAIN SALE

Sometimes, a donor owns an asset but is not in a position to give 100% of it to charity. In this case, it is possible for the donor to contribute part of it and sell part of it. This is called a bargain sale.

A BARGAIN SALE occurs when the donor sells assets to a charity for an amount less than the assets' fair market value. For example, assume you own real estate that a charity would like to own to build on. Perhaps the charity has already asked if you would consider donating it, but you have some cash needs and cannot afford to give it away. The bargain sale would be a win-win in this case. The charity pays you an agreed amount of money (say 20% of the property's value). The difference between the fair market value and the payment you receive is a tax-deductible charitable contribution to the charity.

Bargain sales offer flexibility with regard to gifts to charities by providing the donor with some cash from the sale of the assets to charity. However, bargain sales do not avoid all of the capital gains tax on appreciated assets. Since a bargain sale is part sale and part gift, the donor is responsible for the capital gains tax due on the portion of the transaction that is a sale. In most cases, however, the income tax deduction on the net gift portion may offset the tax effect of the gain portion. When making a bargain sale, the donor receives some cash and a net charitable deduction, eliminates the trouble of trying to sell the property, benefits a charity and avoids a portion of the capital gains tax.

Gifts That Give Back

Many donors don't realize that there are creative ways to support a charity while retaining an income interest for life. The benefit of these plans is that the donor can choose among several gift types in order to achieve the terms and benefits she needs. Following is a general summary of these plans along with some considerations for participating in the right plan.

CHARITABLE GIFT ANNUITIES (CGA)

A charitable gift annuity is appropriate for those who wish to give to charity but have a need for income from their gift. It is an agreement wherein the donor irrevocably transfers cash, securities or real estate (when not prohibited by state law) to the charity. In exchange, the charity pays to the donor (and to another beneficiary if the donor chooses) a fixed income for life based on the age or ages of the annuitants.

The donor receives an immediate income tax deduction for a portion of the gift. The deduction is a function of several variables: the life expectancy of the beneficiaries, the percentage rate paid, the frequency of payments and a prescribed IRS rate for inflation that fluctuates monthly. In general, the charitable deduction for a charitable gift annuity is in the range of 35% to 55% of the value of the gift.

An important benefit of the gift annuity is that a portion of each annuity payment received by the donor is tax free until the donor reaches his or her IRS-determined life expectancy. After reaching that age, payments received are fully taxable as ordinary income. Most charities use the rate schedule suggested by the American Council on Gift Annuities to determine an appropriate payout rate to pay the donors. These rates are fairly standard among charitable organizations, although some charities offer slightly higher or lower rates than those suggested by the American Council on Gift Annuities. Donors should remember that a charity's gift annuity rate will always be lower than the rate for a commercial annuity because there is no charitable element with a commercial annuity.

In addition to the tax benefits, another advantage to charitable gift annuities is the elimination of the estate tax on the assets used to create the charitable gift annuity. Furthermore, a charitable gift annuity is a relatively simple gift vehicle that requires no legal fees for document preparation on the part of the donor.

Funding charitable gift annuities with cash gifts is very common because it is simple and easy to accomplish. Cash gifts also generate a charitable deduction based on the 50% of AGI contribution ceiling. Gifts of appreciated stock or real estate (if not prohibited by state law) held more than a year offer capital gains tax savings as well. If appreciated stock or real estate were sold, capital gains tax generally would have to be paid on the appreciation. On the other hand, if the appreciated asset was transferred to a charity in exchange for a charitable gift annuity, there would be no immediate loss to capital gains taxes; therefore, the donor would receive the fixed rate payment on the full market value of the asset transferred. Part of the capital gains liability is eliminated, and what remains is spread over the donor's life expectancy. Thus, the annuity payment may have up to three tiers of taxability: ordinary income, long-term capital gains and tax-free return of principal. Any charity that offers gift annuities can provide a detailed illustration based on your unique situation.

The Deferred Charitable Gift Annuity

For donors who don't need the income right away, a variation called a Deferred Gift Annuity could work well. The donor agrees to delay the payment for a year or more. In return, the donor receives a higher charitable deduction than would be the case for an immediate payment gift annuity. Also, the rate the charity is able to pay is higher.

Generally, the minimum gift size for a charitable gift annuity is $10,000, but many charities accept gifts of $5,000. A few will accept lower level gifts to this plan.

CHARITABLE REMAINDER TRUST

A charitable remainder trust provides benefits to the donor somewhat similar to those of the gift annuity; however, it is far more flexible for the donor who has unique objectives and goals. Unlike the charitable gift annuity, charitable remainder trusts can be tailored to the donor's needs.

As with the gift annuity, the charitable remainder trust allows the donor the opportunity to irrevocably transfer assets to charity, retain an income stream for life (for self or others), avoid capital gains tax on appreciated long-term property and receive a charitable deduction. The deduction amount is based on age, payout rate, frequency of payments and an inflation factor prescribed by the IRS.

If you intend to make a charitable gift after death, consider making the gift now using a charitable remainder trust to achieve the added benefit of a current income tax deduction. Estate taxes are also reduced because the asset is removed from your taxable estate. These trusts also allow you to convert highly appreciated assets into other investments that may return a higher yield and avoid paying capital gains tax in the process.

Creating a Charitable Remainder Trust

A charitable remainder trust is governed by its trust document, generally drafted by the donor's attorney. Since many charitable organizations run sophisticated charitable giving programs, a charity may be able to give the donor a specimen trust document for review by the donor's own attorney. It is important for a donor to have her own attorney review any plan proposed by a charity.

A charitable remainder trust, with its own tax ID number, is administered by a trustee named in the trust and chosen by the donor. This can be a trust company, brokerage firm or the charity. In many cases, the donor can also be the trustee. However, there are complicated rules governing charitable remainder trusts. Therefore, even if the donor is the trustee, she should consider hiring an administrator to track the transactions and prepare the tax returns.

The donor funds the charitable remainder trust by transferring assets to it. Although the charitable remainder trust works well for cash and securities just like the gift annuity, it is the most appropriate gift for nonliquid assets such as closely held stock, real estate and, occasionally, works of art.

A charitable remainder trust is a tax-exempt entity. Therefore, when the trustee sells the assets at fair market value and reinvests the sales proceeds, there is no immediate capital gains tax liability. Thus, a charitable remainder trust is often used as a charitable gift vehicle when a donor has a large holding of a single stock or investment that needs diversification.

Trust payments may be made to the donor alone or to both the donor and the donor's spouse, and, unlike the charitable gift annuity, a charitable remainder trust can have additional beneficiaries after the death of the original beneficiaries. In addition, a charitable remainder trust can be established for a term of up to 20 years. At the death of the survivor of all beneficiaries, or after the term of years selected by the donor, the trust ends and the trustee transfers the trust assets to one or more charities named in the trust.

Although charitable remainder trusts are irrevocable, the donor may retain some control. For example, the donor may retain the right to change the trustee of the trust or change the charity or charities that receive the remainder of the trust after the death of the beneficiaries. Since this change can be made in the donor's will, she will always have control over which charities will ultimately receive the assets in the trust at termination.

Choosing the Trust Assets

Appreciated property such as stock or real estate provides the greatest tax benefits when used to fund a charitable trust. This is due to the fact that the trust is not required to pay capital gains tax when it sells the assets. Therefore, the lower the basis of the contributed assets, the more capital gains tax savings is available. There can be no written agreement for sale requiring the trust to sell real estate before it is contributed to the trust. You should know that the existence of a mortgage on real estate will create difficulties for a charitable remainder trust. Therefore, if you have mortgaged real estate, consult an attorney familiar with charitable giving tax law before transferring it to a charitable remainder trust.

General Rules

A charitable remainder trust must conform to certain rules and restrictions in order to qualify for favorable tax treatment.

The donor can choose the payout rate upon creating the trust, but the payout must be a minimum of 5% and no greater than 50% of the initial funding amount. Once selected, the payout percentage can never be changed. In addition, the calculation for the amount that will ultimately go to charity must be a minimum of 10%. Therefore, if the beneficiary is too young and the payout is too high, the charitable remainder trust will not pass the 10% test.

In general, a charitable remainder trust operates on a total return concept. Therefore, if the actual income earned is less than the required payment, the trustee makes up the rest of the payment with principal. If income earned is greater than the required payment, the excess is added to principal.

Fixed Payout
(Charitable Remainder Annuity Trust)

There are two basic variations of a charitable remainder trust. The CHARITABLE REMAINDER ANNUITY TRUST (CRAT) pays a fixed amount based on a percentage of the initial funding amount. Once set, the amount of the payment will never change. For example, if a donor funds a CRAT with $100,000 and selects 5%, her annual payment will always be $5,000. Or, if she selects 6%, the payment will always be $6,000. Regardless of the fluctuation in the value of the assets, the payment will not change.

The highest allowable payout rate that meets the 10% remainder test is based on your age and current interest rates. For example, a 50-year-old donor would have a maximum payout of 8%, and a 65-year-old donor would have 10%. The type of payout from an annuity trust may be preferred by older donors who desire a fixed payout amount. (A disadvantage to this approach is that if inflation increases, the fixed payment will have less purchasing power in the future.) In addition, the annuity trust can never receive an additional gift after its initial funding.

Variable Payout
(Charitable Remainder Unitrust)

The second type of charitable remainder trust is called a CHARITABLE REMAINDER UNITRUST (CRUT). With this trust, you choose the percentage payout rate that you wish just as you would with a CRAT. The difference is that a CRUT must have its assets revalued every year and the chosen payout rate is multiplied times this annual value to determine the trust's payment for that year. The CRUT pays a fixed percentage of the trust assets as determined every year. At the time the trust is initially funded, the percentage payout rate is multiplied by the value of the trust assets to determine the payment you will receive for that year only. The payment in future years will fluctuate based on the investment performance as reflected in the annual value of the trust. The trust is revalued on the same date each year, and each year's income paid out is determined by multiplying the chosen percentage payout rate times the value of the trust.

If you established your CRUT in 2004 with $100,000 and chose a 6% payout rate, your income for the year 2004 would be $6,000. However, if on January 1, 2005, the trust value was $110,000, your income for 2005 would be $6,600 ($110,000 x 6%). Although the percent is fixed, the income received may increase or decrease over time as the trust assets grow or shrink. Standard unitrust rules require that if not enough interest and dividends are earned by the CRUT to provide the amount required to be distributed, any shortfall must be made up by invading the principal of the CRUT.

A Charitable Remainder Trust for Nonliquid Assets

Due to the mandatory payout requirement for the two types of charitable remainder trusts discussed on these two pages, the assets most commonly used to fund them are cash and marketable securities. The payout must be made on time, and there would be serious difficulties if either the annuity trust or standard unitrust were funded with nonliquid assets such as real estate or closely held stock that were not earning sufficient income to satisfy the payment requirements.

However, another type of charitable remainder unitrust, known as a flip trust, is an alternative vehicle for nonliquid assets. The flip unitrust provides for the payment of "net income" (which might also mean no income if the trust assets pay no income) during the time that the trustee attempts to dispose of the real estate or other nonincome-producing asset. In general, after the trustee successfully sells the nonliquid asset and reinvests the proceeds, the trust "flips" to become a standard unitrust as described above. The flip unitrust can also be drafted to have a "net income" payment until a particular event such as marriage, divorce, death or birth of a child, called the "flip triggering event." As with all other life income plans, the assets are distributed to one or more charities at the death of the beneficiaries or at the end of the trust term.

Income Tax Benefits of Charitable Remainder Trusts

A donor who funds a charitable remainder trust receives a charitable income tax deduction in the year of the gift for a portion of the value of the gift. Certain variables including the beneficiary's life expectancy, the payout rate, an inflation factor and frequency of payments are used to determine what value will ultimately go to charity.

The charitable deduction is higher with a 5% payout than with an 8% payout. Also, the deduction increases as the beneficiary gets older. Bear in mind that the charitable deduction is the figure that must pass the 10% test in order for the charitable remainder trust to be qualified. Therefore, if your life expectancy is too long in conjunction with the payout rate, the trust might fail. Your attorney can adjust the terms of the trust to ensure that your trust qualifies. He or she can lower the payout or set the trust term for a period of years, and that should do it.

As with outright gifts, the charitable contribution ceilings are the same. The income tax deduction for contributions of appreciated assets to the trust is limited to 30% of the donor's contribution base. For gifts of cash, the limit is 50% of the donor's contribution base. In both cases, any excess can be carried forward and deducted for the subsequent five years.

Taxation of Payments From Charitable Remainder Trusts

One of the more advantageous features of a charitable remainder trust is that the payments to the beneficiaries receive preferential tax treatment. Rather than being all ordinary income, which could be taxed up to 35%, the payments from a charitable remainder trust could be taxed at lower rates.

In general, the trustee pays out categories of income in the order of highest to lowest taxation. Therefore, based on the actual performance of the charitable remainder trust, the makeup of the beneficiary payment is 1) ordinary income, 2) long-term capital gains income, 3) tax-exempt income and 4) tax-free return of principal.

For the most part, donors generally receive some of their payments as ordinary income and some as capital gain. The good news is that some dividends that formerly would have been taxed at the highest 35% income tax bracket are now taxed at 15%. The trustee of your charitable remainder trust will send you a K-1 tax form at the end of each year informing you of the exact amounts of income in each category.

Who Should Consider Using Charitable Remainder Trusts?

Charitable remainder trusts are very versatile. Therefore, a charitable remainder trust is an excellent gift for many situations. Among them are the following:

• Donor wants to benefit more than one charity.

• Donor wants to retain the right to change the charity.

• Donor has a large block of highly appreciated stock and would like to diversify without incurring an immediate capital gains tax.

- Donor has nonliquid assets such as real estate or closely held stock.

- Donor wants to retain some control over the management of the assets.

- Donor wants to do something for her favorite charity but cannot afford to give up the income.

Due to the expense of drafting and managing a charitable remainder trust, it is generally advisable for the donor to consider a minimum gift size of $100,000 to fund a charitable remainder trust.

Several years ago, Hannah established her charitable remainder unitrust. It is a standard unitrust, and this year the trust has a required payout of $6,000, which Hannah receives. How Hannah reports the $6,000 on her income tax return depends upon the nature of the payment distributed by the trust. If the trust had only $2,000 of ordinary income for the year and had no undistributed ordinary income from prior years, then $2,000 of the $6,000 would be taxed to Hannah as ordinary income. In addition to the ordinary income, if the trust had capital gains of another $3,000 during the year, then $3,000 of her $6,000 would be taxed as capital gains income. If the trustee had invested in some tax-free municipal bonds and those bonds earned income of $500, then the $500 received by Hannah would be received as tax-exempt income. The final $500 received by Hannah would be considered a tax-free distribution of principal if the trust did not earn enough from ordinary income, capital gains or tax-exempt income to generate the $6,000 necessary to distribute to Hannah.

Replacing Charitable Trust Assets With a Wealth Replacement Trust

Donors who wish to help a favorite charity are often unable to do so because they worry about giving away assets intended for their heirs. Wealth replacement trusts are a common strategy to address this concern. The increased income provided to the donor from the charitable remainder trust, or from another life income plan, can be used to pay the premium on a life insurance policy that is structured to replace the value of the donated assets. In general, the donor creates a life insurance trust (LIT) with the heir or heirs as beneficiaries. Each year, the donor transfers money to the life insurance trust. In turn, the life insurance trust buys life insurance on the donor's life. If properly structured, the entire proceeds of the life insurance trust will pass to the heirs completely free of estate tax.

This strategy is an alternative for the donor worried about disinheriting someone. On the death of the donor, the assets in the charitable remainder trust are distributed to charity, and the life insurance proceeds in the life insurance trust are distributed to the heir or heirs. Older donors in reasonably good health will be surprised to know that they are not too old to buy life insurance.

POOLED INCOME FUNDS

For donors who don't have the resources necessary to create a charitable remainder trust, the pooled income fund is an alternative. A pooled income fund works like a mutual fund run by the charity. Gifts from all donors are invested together. Then, each donor receives a share of the fund's annual income for life. Upon the death of the beneficiary(ies), the investments remaining in the fund are distributed to the sponsoring charity.

Pooled income funds pay all ordinary income unlike charitable remainder trusts which pay income in up to four categories. For smaller donors ($5,000 to $10,000), the pooled income fund is an economical vehicle through which to make a gift and receive income.

Similar to the gift annuity and the charitable remainder trust, a pooled income fund allows a donor to contribute highly appreciated assets without loss to capital gains taxes. As a result, the full value of the assets are available to earn income for the donor.

In addition, the donor receives a current income tax deduction for a portion of the gift. The deduction is based on age, yield of the fund and frequency of payments. Although it is impossible to know year to year how much income you will receive, charities that run pooled income funds can provide information about their historical returns and investment strategy for the fund.

Cash and marketable securities work equally well to fund a pooled income fund gift. In general, a pooled income fund needs quick liquidity of the assets contributed. Therefore, real estate or closely held stock is inappropriate.

CHARITABLE BEQUESTS FROM WILLS AND LIVING TRUSTS

Often donors enjoy making gifts during their lifetimes because they see the benefit of their gifts put to work while they are alive. However, others are not in a position to part with assets that they might need currently or for retirement. Fortunately, there are several ways to make gifts through wills or living trusts which are flexible and can be tailored to the donors' needs.

1. General Bequest: The donor specifies a dollar amount (for example, "$5,000 to my church.")

2. Specific Bequest: A donor gives specific assets to charity such as "my hunting cabin" or "my shore property" or specific stocks and bonds.

3. Percentage Bequest: The donor gives a percentage of the total estate to charity (for example, "10% of the value of my estate to the Boys & Girls Club.")

4. Residual Bequest: The donor specifies that the residual estate goes to one or more charities. This would be the case if one desired to donate to charity what is left of the estate after taxes, expenses and family needs are fulfilled.

It is very important that the bequest language include the exact legal name of the charity and its complete address. In addition, the bequest language may include any specific purposes for the gift or restrictions on its use.

CHARITABLE LEAD TRUSTS

The CHARITABLE LEAD TRUST is the reverse of the charitable remainder trust with respect to how the payments are made. While the charitable remainder trust pays income to the donor for life and pays the remainder to charity at the donor's death, the charitable lead trust pays income first to the charity for a term of years, and the remainder is paid back to the donor or intended beneficiaries. This means that the charity leads the interest of the noncharitable recipient.

The most common use of a charitable lead trust is to pass assets to her heirs and family at a greatly reduced gift or estate tax cost. Charitable lead trusts can be established either during one's lifetime or after death. Some donors set up charitable lead trust in order to support a charity's capital campaign for a period of years.

Foundations

PRIVATE FOUNDATIONS

A private foundation is essentially a private tax-exempt organization whose purpose is to benefit charities, educational institutions or other nonprofit organizations of the donor's choosing. As a charitable organization, contributions to a private foundation qualify for tax deductions. Tax deduction limits for gifts to a private foundation are more restrictive than for gifts to a public charity. Gifts of cash to a private foundation may be deducted only up to 30% of the donor's adjusted gross income. Gifts of appreciated assets may only be deducted up to 20% of the donor's adjusted gross income. For a public charity, these limits are 50% for cash contributions and 30% for appreciated assets. For both types of charities, any excess deductions may be carried forward for five years. Private foundations do not provide charitable services but make grants to provide funding to qualified charities. Individuals and corporations have established more than 50,000 private foundations. They each are created and controlled by a single source of funds (usually one individual or family) and not the general public. Private foundations are established to provide a greater degree of control to the donor and her family than is possible for public charities. The donor retains substantial control over administration and investment of the assets donated to the private foundation.

Another reason that donors use private foundations is that they are excellent vehicles by which to transfer the donor's values to the next generation. This is accomplished by involving the younger generation in the administration and management of the foundation and its grants. Another advantage of private foundations is that the tax deduction is taken in the year of donations, but the amount contributed can be distributed to charities over the course of many years. The governing form of a private foundation can be either a trust or a nonprofit corporation. Once the organization has been established and the board of directors or trustees appointed, the IRS requires additional documentation.

Private foundations must generally distribute at least 5% of their net investment assets to qualified charities each year. Establishing a foundation and complying with its reporting requirements incurs ongoing legal and accounting expenses. Private foundations are appropriate for those who want control over the investment of the donated assets, as well as involvement in the making of grants for charitable purposes. They also provide the donor with recognition and publicity. Donors who establish private foundations can use them to channel all of the charitable giving of all family members into one vehicle. This would result in larger gifts for greater impact on charities.

COMMUNITY FOUNDATIONS

Community foundations are classified by the IRS as public charities. They are organized as a permanent collection of endowed funds for the long-term benefit of a defined geographic area. Establishing a fund or account at a community foundation achieves many of the same charitable objectives as a private foundation but is far less costly to administer.

> There are a number of advantages to community foundations. Contributors may deduct contributions up to 50% of their adjusted gross income. Another advantage is that the donor's fund is exempt from filing its own tax return since its financial transactions are consolidated with those of other funds on the community foundation's tax return. These advantages, in addition to the wide latitude in choices in the naming of endowed funds, make the community foundation a popular choice for many donors.

The governing body of a community foundation is made up of representatives of the general public. Like private foundations, they operate primarily as grant-making organizations. Grants are made from each fund of a community foundation in accordance with the instructions the donor gave to the community foundation when she established the fund.

Community foundations accept gifts of cash and other assets typically with a minimum value of $5,000. Donors to community foundations generally have the option to contribute to any of at least three different types of funds:

1. Unrestricted Fund: The community foundation has complete discretion to make grants as it sees fit.

2. Field of Interest Fund: The community foundation allows the donor to designate special interest areas to receive grants such as the environment, arts, education or health. The community foundation makes discretionary grants to charities serving these fields of interest.

3. Donor-Advised Fund: The donor may recommend that grants be made in specific amounts to specific qualified charities from funds contributed by the donor. A donor-advised fund at a community foundation is an alternative to a private foundation, by allowing the donor to come under the tax and accounting umbrella of a public charity. Those who want to be actively involved in grant making may designate this type of fund. In effect, the donor becomes an advisor. The community foundation, however, has final authority as to whether the donor's recommendation is approved. Contributions to community foundations are advised when a donor desires to have input as to the selection of charities in a specific geographic area.

DONOR-ADVISED FUNDS

Community foundations are not the only charitable organizations that offer the flexibility of a donor-advised fund. A number of national financial institutions have established public charities that offer donor-advised funds. As with the community foundation, the donor-advised funds associated with national financial institutions allow the donor to make an irrevocable gift to the fund, secure a tax deduction for the value of the contribution in the year of the gift and yet take years to make grants. Donors enjoy having accounts named after their families and the simplification of having grants forwarded by the fund upon their request. The donor receives periodic statements concerning the value of the account and grants paid from it.

Most donor-advised funds only accept gifts of liquid assets such as cash or securities. If a donor contributes appreciated stock (that has been owned for longer than a year), she gets an income tax deduction for the full fair market value of the stock and also avoids any capital gains tax on the appreciation.

Although contributions to the fund must be managed by the fund, the donor does become an advisor as to the amount and timing of grants from the donor's account. Grants are restricted to go only to qualified charities and must be consistent with the guidelines established by the board of directors of the donor-advised fund.

Donor-advised funds offered by national financial institutions differ from those offered by community foundations in two important aspects. First, the financial institutions impose few, if any, geographic limitations on the recipients of the grants. Second, they do not have in-house expertise relating to the charitable needs within local communities.

Typical donor-advised funds permit the donor to establish her own named fund (i.e., The Jones Fund) in the form of an account registered with the financial institution. The donor recommends the qualified charity and how much it should receive. Normally, the fund would have a $250 minimum gift amount. The donor-advised fund has the legal right to reject recommendations.

Minimum initial contributions range from $10,000 to $50,000, with additional contributions made in smaller amounts. All administration is handled by the fund, and any growth of the fund is tax free. Since the balance in the fund is hopefully growing on a tax-free basis, this would perhaps result in a larger amount given to charity, although the full amount of the tax deduction cannot be increased. There are management fees to be paid with such funds, and they should be discussed carefully before using the services of any fund sponsored by a financial institution.

Donor-advised funds are appropriate for those who support multiple charities and like the idea of using a single fund to make all their grants. These funds are also appropriate for those who want to support charities without regard to geographic limitations and would like to make charitable contributions now for income tax purposes but want to have the option to consider which charities should receive the amount contributed and control the timing of the gifts.

One advantage of the donor-advised fund over the private foundation is that tax deductions are limited to 30% of the donor's contribution base for contributions to private foundations, whereas contributions to a donor-advised fund qualify for an income tax deduction of up to 50% of the donor's contribution base.

Compared to private foundations, donor-advised funds have a number of advantages:

1. There are no startup fees for donor-advised funds, while the startup fees and administrative expenses of a private foundation can be significant.

2. There are no annual requirements for distributions from donor-advised funds. Private foundations are required to distribute 5% of the net asset value of the foundation each year.

3. Excise taxes of approximately 2% of annual income are required to be paid by private foundations; no such requirement is necessary for donor-advised funds.

4. The tax return for a private foundation is a public record (form PF-990) while donors may choose to remain anonymous as to the recipient of any grants made from their donor-advised fund.

Summary

The material regarding charitable estate planning is one of the most important chapters of this book. Although we have considered the legal and technical aspects, such as what is a gift and what is a charity, the more important consideration is transferring your values to succeeding generations. Charitable giving allows you to leave a legacy of giving to those you love, as well as financial benefits to those individuals and organizations you care about.

The combination of women's attitudes toward giving, tax benefits and the many strategies available to help others have a better life makes charitable estate planning a particularly exciting pursuit for women. The next step is to discover how to use this information to pay zero estate tax.

Step 8

Discover How To Pay Zero Estate Tax

Topics Include

Who Must Pay the Federal Estate Tax?

Estate Tax Rates

Estate Tax Deductions and Credits

An Overview of the Gift Tax

Five Key Strategies to Pay Zero Estate Tax

Introduction

On June 7, 2001, President Bush signed into law the Economic Growth and Tax Relief Reconciliation Act of 2001, known as the Tax Relief Act of 2001. This law significantly revised the federal estate and gift tax laws. The new law increased the amount that can be left to heirs free of estate tax to $1,500,000 for the years 2004 and 2005, with a graduated exclusion scale reaching $3,500,000 for estate tax purposes in 2009.

There is an interesting "sunset" provision contained in this law, however, that makes the entire law expire on December 31, 2010. Of course, new legislation could extend the repeal date, but unless a new law is enacted by December 31, 2010, the estate and gift tax law will revert to that which was in existence prior to the Tax Relief Act of 2001.

Who Must Pay the Estate Tax?

The estate tax considers both the value of your assets and the year of your death to determine if any tax is due. Your estate must pay the tax only if its value on the date of your passing is greater than your lifetime exclusion amount (also known as APPLICABLE EXCLUSION AMOUNT, UNIFIED CREDIT AMOUNT and ESTATE TAX EXEMPTION). The table below shows the lifetime exclusion amounts established by the Tax Relief Act of 2001.

Lifetime Exclusions

Year of Death	Estate Tax Lifetime Exclusion	Unified Tax Credit	Gift Tax Lifetime Exclusion	Highest Estate & Gift Tax Rates
2004	$1.5 million	$555,800	$1 million	48%
2005	$1.5 million	$555,800	$1 million	47%
2006	$2 million	$780,800	$1 million	46%
2007	$2 million	$780,800	$1 million	45%
2008	$2 million	$780,800	$1 million	45%
2009	$3.5 million	$1,250,800	$1 million	45%
2010	Unlimited (Taxes Repealed)	—	$1 million	35% (Gift Tax Only)
2011 & after	$1 million	$345,800	$1 million	55%

What Are the Tax Rates?

If your estate is valued at less than your lifetime exclusion amount, then no federal estate tax will be due upon your death. Only estates with values greater than the lifetime exclusion amount are required to pay federal estate tax.

The tax is calculated by first determining the tax due on your entire estate without considering your lifetime exclusion amount. The amount due on your entire estate is known as the gross tax due. Next, an amount known as the UNIFIED TAX CREDIT is subtracted from the gross tax due. The net amount represents the tax due for your estate. The unified tax credit reduces the estate tax liability dollar for dollar. The maximum amount that can pass tax free due to this tax credit reduction is equal to its equivalent lifetime exclusion amount.

Federal Estate and Gift Tax Rates			
Size of Taxable Estate	Base Amount	Base Tax	Plus % on Excess over Base
$1,500,001–$2,000,000	$1,500,000	$555,800	45%
Over $2,000,000	$2,000,000	$780,800	48%*

* The maximum rate of tax is scheduled to be lowered. See chart on previous page.

How to Calculate the Federal Estate Tax

First, determine the total value of all assets owned by the decedent on her date of death. This is known as her "gross estate." From this total amount, subtract any debts that she owed to others. Additional deductions are permitted for expenses incurred in settling the estate. These are legal and accounting fees, funeral expenses and grave marker, for example. After the deductions are subtracted from the gross estate, the resulting value is known as the "net taxable estate."

Second, compute the "tentative tax" using the appropriate federal estate tax rate. This is the tax that would be due if there was no lifetime exclusion amount.

Lastly, subtract the "unified tax credit" for the year of death from the tentative tax. The unified tax credit equals the amount of estate tax that would be due if there was no lifetime exclusion amount. The resulting dollar amount after subtracting the "unified tax credit" from the "tentative tax" is the actual federal estate tax due.

Martha's Estate Tax Calculation

Martha was widowed in her 30s and started a cleaning service to support herself and her two children. Her small business grew until she had 15 cleaning crews and a growing estate. Upon her untimely death in the year 2005, Martha's estate consisted of:

Asset	Value	-	Loans	=	Net Estate Value
Auto	$30,000		($10,000)		$20,000
House	$300,000		($200,000)		$100,000
IRA	$150,000		$0		$150,000
Business	$1,500,000		$0		$1,500,000
Investments	$300,000		$0		$300,000
Personal Property	$50,000		$0		$50,000
TOTALS	$2,330,000	-	$210,000	=	$2,120,000

Martha's net estate is $2,120,000. The tentative tax on $2,120,000 from the estate tax rate chart is calculated by determining that the size of the estate is "over $2,000,000." According to the chart, then, the tentative tax is determined by a multi-step process.

1. First, the "base amount" is $2,000,000. The base tax on $2,000,000 is $780,800.

2. The next step is to calculate the tax on the remaining $120,000 by multiplying this amount by the tax rate for 2005 of 47%. The result is $56,400.

3. Next, add the base tax of $780,800 to the amount of $56,400. Thus, the total tentative tax is $837,200.

4. Now that the tentative tax has been calculated, the final step is to subtract the unified tax credit which for 2005 is $555,800. Therefore, $837,200 minus $555,800 results in the actual tax due of $281,400.

Assets Included in Your Gross Estate at Death

To be taxed, the assets included in your gross estate must be both owned by you at the time of death and transferred to another. The following are examples of assets included in your estate for estate tax purposes:

- Real Estate: residential, vacation property, farm or business real estate

- Bank Accounts: checking, savings, CDs, money market funds

- Financial Assets: stocks, bonds, treasury bills, mutual funds

- Money Loaned to Others: notes, mortgages, installment sales

- Business Assets: equipment, tools, machinery

- Closely Held Businesses: partnerships, limited liability companies, closely-held stock

- Personal Property: automobiles, trucks, furniture, guns, antiques, and collectibles

- Retirement Plans: IRAs, 401(k)s, Keoghs

- Annuities

- Life Insurance: Proceeds of life insurance on your life are included in your estate only if they are paid to your estate or you owned the policy.

- Jointly Owned Assets: The full value of all assets owned as joint tenants with rights of survivorship is included in the gross estate of the first joint owner to die. (The estate tax has an exception to this rule for assets owned jointly by husband and wife. In that case, only half of the value of the joint assets is taxed in the estate of the first to die.)

Valuing the Gross Estate

Once all of the assets of the estate are identified, valuing the gross estate is the next step. Since the value of the estate determines the tax, an important element of estate planning is to accurately value your assets.

All assets are valued at the fair market value as of the date of death. Fair market value is the price at which a willing buyer would buy and a willing seller would sell the assets, both having reasonable knowledge of all relevant facts and neither under any compulsion to buy or sell. There is an exception to the requirement of valuing assets as of the date of death. It is known as the ALTERNATE VALUATION DATE. This is a date six months after the date of death. Assets can be valued as of that date only if using that value results in both a lower gross estate and lower estate taxes. This is commonly done. For example, if somebody held a large stock portfolio on the date of her death and six months later the stock market fell in value, her stocks would be worth a lot less. Under these circumstances, using the alternative valuation date to value the stocks would result in lower taxes.

Estate Tax Deductions and Credits

Once the assets comprising your gross estate are identified and valued, a number of deductions are permitted:

- Debts and Unpaid Mortgages

- Estate Settlement Expenses: Including administrative and funeral expenses, executor's fees, attorney's fees, and interest

- Charitable Deduction: This deduction is for the value of assets transferred by your estate to qualified charities. It does not apply if gifts are made by your heirs and are not specified in your estate plan.

- Marital Deduction: If you are married on the date of your death, this deduction is for the value of all assets passing to your surviving spouse.

- State Death Tax Credit: This tax credit equals the value of inheritance taxes paid to states. The state death tax credit is currently being phased out and will be terminated beginning in 2005. In its place will be a deduction from the value of the gross estate equal to the amount of state inheritance taxes paid.

Liquidity Planning

A significant challenge when planning for the federal estate tax is finding the cash necessary to pay it. The tax is due within nine months of the date of death, and the IRS generally requires immediate payment in full. There are three sources of money to pay the tax if there is not enough money in your estate:

1. SELL ESTATE ASSETS

Money could be raised to pay the tax by selling estate assets. Forced sales are generally to be avoided because they could result in receiving sales proceeds that are far below the fair market value of the assets being sold.

2. BORROW THE MONEY FROM THE BANK OR BENEFICIARIES

This presumes the estate has the capacity to borrow the money for, perhaps, a 10-year period at reasonable interest rates. Like forced liquidation of assets, borrowing money from the bank to pay the tax is an expensive alternative, and beneficiaries seldom have the ability or desire to loan money to an estate.

3. PURCHASE LIFE INSURANCE

In many cases, the optimal choice to provide the liquidity necessary to pay the taxes is to purchase life insurance during your lifetime to cover these costs.

Overview of the Gift Tax

Whenever assets are given to another for less than full value, the amount by which the value of the assets exceeds the money paid for them is a gift. Although the Tax Relief Act of 2001 carries a provision to repeal the federal estate tax, there is no repeal of the gift tax, and the gift tax top rate becomes 35% in the year 2010.

Who Must Pay the Gift Tax?

The gift tax affects gifts that exceed the gift tax ANNUAL EXCLUSION AMOUNT. This amount is $11,000, and it is adjusted for inflation. Therefore, if you give $11,000 or less to any one person in any given year, there is no gift tax. Gifts made to anyone, regardless of their relationship to you, qualify for the annual exclusion amount.

In addition to the $11,000 gift exclusion for individuals, husbands and wives may split gifts between them. For example, if a husband wanted to give a $22,000 gift to his nephew, his wife could join in the gift and there would be no gift tax due because it would be deemed to be a $11,000 gift from the husband and a $11,000 gift from his wife. There is also an unlimited marital deduction on gifts made by one spouse to the other so long as each spouse is a U.S. citizen.

In addition to the $11,000 annual exclusion, there is an unlimited exclusion for payments made for educational tuition expense and medical expenses. The amounts paid for educational tuition and medical expenses must be paid directly to the educational institution or the medical provider.

A gift can be any type of asset and still qualify for the $11,000 annual exclusion. It does not need to be cash. For example, if Mother and Father own a farm valued at $800,000, they can gift a partial interest in the farm to their son by conveying to him by deed an $11,000 interest from Father and an $11,000 interest from Mother for a total $22,000 interest in the farm. This would be a deed transferring 2.75% of the farm ($22,000 ÷ $800,000). An additional portion of the farm could be conveyed if a discount is applied to the value of the gift due to its lack of marketability.

How the Gift Tax Interacts With the Estate Tax

If you give over $11,000 to any one person in one year, the amount exceeding $11,000 will reduce your federal estate tax lifetime exclusion amount. Once you have made gifts to one individual in excess of the total of both your $11,000 annual exclusion amount and your $1,000,000 lifetime gift tax exclusion amount (for 2004), you must pay gift tax on the value of the gifts in excess of this total.

If a gift tax return is due, it generally must be filed *no later than April 15 of the calendar year following the year of the gift.* If the assets being gifted are hard to value (such as farmland, real estate or unlisted stock), it must be appraised so that the value of the gift can be confirmed.

The Generous Mother Plans Ahead

If Janet gave her daughter, Jane, $50,000, a gift tax return would be required to be filed. The gift tax return would show that of the $50,000 gift from Janet to Jane, $11,000 qualified for the annual exclusion amount. The remaining $39,000 in gift will reduce Janet's federal estate tax lifetime exclusion amount to $961,000 ($1,000,000 - $39,000 = $961,000). Unlike the increasing exclusion scale for the estate tax, the lifetime exclusion amount for gifts remains at $1,000,000 indefinitely.

The Generation-Skipping Transfer Tax

When the federal estate tax was imposed, families began to avoid it by making gifts to their grandchildren instead of to their children. This strategy avoided the tax that would occur when their children would transfer the same wealth to their grandchildren. They could thereby skip a generation. The government responded to this planning technique, and the Tax Reform Act of 1986 instituted the generation-skipping transfer (GST) tax. This is a tax imposed upon the value of assets transferred from one generation to a succeeding generation, only if it skips a generation in between. The tax is designed to produce the same result as though the estate tax had been imposed on the transfer to each successive generation.

A generation-skipping transfer occurs when any transfer of assets skips a generation. Skips can be direct skips, where assets are left directly to grandchildren, or an indirect skip where assets are transferred into a trust for the benefit of a child, and only upon the child's death are trust assets transferred to grandchildren.

There is an exemption from the generation-skipping transfer tax. The exemption is indexed for inflation and is currently $1,500,000. The tax rate is the same as the highest estate tax rate on amounts transferred in excess of the lifetime exemption amount.

How to Pay Zero Estate Tax

We will now look at five primary estate tax planning strategies. Not all of these strategies may apply to you. On the other hand, your estate may be large enough to justify an approach more complex than the strategies discussed here. Nevertheless, these are the five strategies that must be addressed before pushing ahead into more complex planning.

Strategy Number One: Maximize the Unlimited Marital Deduction

The unlimited marital deduction is applied to estate assets that pass from the deceased spouse to the surviving spouse. The first spouse to pass away must be a U.S. citizen or a resident of the United States. In addition, the surviving spouse must be a citizen of the United States to qualify for the unlimited marital deduction. If the surviving spouse is not a U.S. citizen, a limited marital deduction is permitted by using what is known as a QUALIFIED DOMESTIC TRUST.

MARITAL DEDUCTION TRUSTS

Assets transferring directly to the surviving spouse qualify for the marital deduction. In addition to direct transfer, there are a number of trusts that qualify for the marital deduction when the deceased spouse transfers assets into a trust. These trusts are known as MARITAL TRUSTS and include the power of appointment trust, the Q-TIP TRUST and the qualified domestic trust.

Power of Appointment Trust

The power of appointment trust allows the surviving spouse the greatest control over how trust assets will be distributed after her death. A trust will qualify as a power of appointment trust so long as the surviving spouse is entitled to all the income at least annually for life. In addition, no person other than the surviving spouse may receive a distribution from the trust during the surviving spouse's lifetime. The surviving spouse must have a general power to appoint the assets to anyone after her death. This means that the surviving spouse may specify in her will or living trust who shall receive the remaining assets in the trust after her death. In addition, the surviving spouse may be given the right to make gifts from the power of appointment trust during her lifetime. The power of appointment trust also permits the trustee to pay as much of the principal to the surviving spouse as the trustee deems advisable or as requested by the surviving spouse.

The power of appointment trust is often used when a spouse believes that if she were to die first, the surviving spouse does not have the experience or desire to manage trust assets. In order to provide management for trust assets, this spouse establishes a power of appointment trust that permits the surviving spouse to distribute trust assets to whomever she chooses when he dies. If the surviving spouse does not name the new trust beneficiaries in her will or living trust, as permitted by the trust, the distribution plan in the power of appointment trust will be effective.

Q-TIP Trust

Q-TIP stands for QUALIFIED TERMINAL INTEREST PROPERTY. This trust is similar to the power of appointment trust. The main difference is that the surviving spouse does not have the power to change the ultimate distribution regarding who receives the Q-TIP trust assets after her death. The surviving spouse must receive all of the income at least annually for life from the Q-TIP trust. Unlike the power of appointment trust, the assets cannot be controlled by the will or living trust of the surviving spouse. The first spouse established the terms regarding who receives the trust assets after the death of the surviving spouse, and no one else may have a power of appointment over trust assets during the surviving spouse's lifetime. This trust is used more than the power of appointment trust.

Another significant difference between the power of appointment trust and the Q-TIP trust is that the power of appointment trust automatically qualifies for the marital deduction, whereas a Q-TIP election must be made to qualify all or only a portion of the Q-TIP trust for the marital deduction. This gives the executor options with regard to postmortem estate planning. The Q-TIP trust is used when one spouse wishes to provide for independent management of trust assets for the surviving spouse as well as control the final disposition of trust assets upon the surviving spouse's death.

Depending upon the decedent's wishes, the trustee may or may not be given the option to invade principal for the benefit of the surviving spouse. Since the entire value of the Q-TIP trust is included in the surviving spouse's estate at her death, there are no limitations on invading principal for her benefit. Full access to principal may be provided to the surviving spouse for any reason. If the purpose of the Q-TIP trust is to protect the ultimate beneficiaries' interest (deceased spouse's children from a prior marriage, for example), then the provisions to invade the principal should be restricted.

Since the federal estate tax lifetime exclusion amount is increasing to $3.5 million, and full repeal is scheduled for the year 2010, Q-TIP trusts may not be necessary in many estates solely for estate tax planning purposes. Q-TIP trusts, however, will continue to be an important estate planning tool for those who wish to provide income to the surviving spouse while protecting the principal for the decedent's beneficiaries.

Forget It, Larry

Wendy's first husband and the father of her two sons died years ago. Wendy remarried, but had no children with her second husband. As a successful investor, Wendy was concerned about what would happen to her estate upon her death, and subsequently, her husband's estate. While her husband had no children, he did have a brother, Larry. When her husband dies, Wendy wants her estate to pass to her sons, not to Larry; therefore, Wendy set up a Q-TIP trust to specify where and to whom her assets go after she and her second husband die.

Qualified Domestic Trust

In the late 1980s, Congress was concerned with the possibility that a U.S. citizen would die, leaving his entire estate to his non-U.S.-citizen spouse, who could then use the marital deduction and take the assets back to her native country. In this scenario, the estate would never be taxed. In 1988, Congress changed the estate tax law to correct this problem. Now, in order for the marital deduction to apply for non-U.S.-citizen surviving spouses, a special type of trust must be used as a marital trust. This trust is known as a qualified domestic trust or Q-DOT.

This trust is only necessary if the first spouse that dies has an estate greater than that year's lifetime exclusion amount. For example, a woman is a U.S. citizen and has assets registered solely in her name equal to $1,500,000. She dies in 2004 and gives everything to her husband. Since her total estate is equal to her lifetime exclusion amount, this amount is permitted to be distributed directly to her noncitizen spouse and still qualify for the unlimited marital deduction. On the other hand, if the value of his assets is greater than his lifetime exclusion amount, the only way to qualify for the marital deduction and thereby avoid paying federal estate tax is to transfer his assets into a qualified domestic trust. At least one trustee of the qualified domestic trust must be a United States citizen or a domestic corporation.

SHOULD THE TRANSFER TO YOUR SURVIVING SPOUSE BE OUTRIGHT OR IN TRUST?

There are a number of factors to consider when making the decision whether to transfer assets directly to your surviving spouse or transfer them into a trust for his benefit:

1. Estate Size: If the total estate of both spouses does not warrant planning for the federal estate tax, the use of a marital trust for tax purposes would not be needed.

2. Citizenship of the Spouses: The qualified domestic trust is required to preserve the marital deduction on assets passing to a noncitizen spouse. If the total estate of husband and

wife is greater than the lifetime exclusion amount, the qualified domestic trust is needed if one is not a U.S. citizen.

3. Management Abilities of the Surviving Spouse: Even if no federal estate tax planning is needed, there may be concern about the ability of the surviving spouse to manage assets previously controlled by the deceased spouse. In this situation, a Q-TIP trust or power of appointment trust should be considered. This would permit a qualified trustee to manage trust assets for the benefit of the surviving spouse and still qualify for the marital deduction.

4. Possible Remarriage of the Surviving Spouse: If the first spouse to die leaves everything outright to the surviving spouse (and the surviving spouse remarries), it is possible that upon the death of the surviving spouse, the new spouse would receive the inheritance and the children of the deceased spouse would be disinherited.

Strategy Number Two: A Credit Shelter Trust "Saves" the Lifetime Exclusion Amount of the First Spouse to Die

Every U.S. citizen has a lifetime exclusion amount. This is the amount that can pass free of federal estate tax at death. Since a husband and wife each have their own lifetime exclusion amounts, in the year 2004 each can pass $1,500,000 tax free to their heirs for a total tax-free transfer of $3,000,000. Unfortunately, if no prior planning is done, there is a catch to this lifetime exclusion amount for married taxpayers: If it is not used during lifetime or at death, it is lost.

The primary benefit of the credit shelter trust (also known as a BYPASS TRUST or an AB TRUST) is the federal estate tax savings it offers. If a husband and wife have each established a credit shelter trust in their wills or living trusts (and have appropriately registered their assets), they can together transfer up to $3,000,000 to their family and heirs with no federal estate tax if they both die in either 2004 or 2005. The lifetime exclusion amount is scheduled to increase: By the year 2009, a husband and wife will be able to transfer up to $7,000,000 to the next generation with no federal estate tax, provided they engage in planning.

How Credit Shelter Trusts Are Established

Credit shelter trust language can be written into either a will or living trust. Since no one knows which spouse will pass away first, the language is placed in each spouse's will or living trust. The will or living trust of the first spouse to die is the only one that will have its credit shelter trust established, since the trust is always established for the benefit of a surviving spouse. When the surviving spouse passes away, no credit

Use It or Lose It

Bill and Estelle had been married for 30 years and had grown their estate to $3,000,000 when Bill suddenly passed away in 2004. Bill's will directed his entire estate to be given to Estelle. There were no federal estate taxes on Bill's assets transferred to Estelle because they qualified for the marital deduction.

Unfortunately, Bill's $1,500,000 lifetime exclusion amount was lost because he never used it during his lifetime, nor did he create an estate plan to utilize it after his death. As a result, when Estelle dies, she can pass only $1,500,000 of the estate (the amount of her lifetime exclusion) tax free to her heirs (if she dies in 2004 or 2005). This would result in over $500,000 in federal estate taxes that could have been avoided.

By sheltering Bill's lifetime exclusion amount in a credit shelter trust, Bill and Estelle together would have been able to pass their $3,000,000 estate tax free to their children.

shelter trust is necessary in order to take advantage of the full lifetime exclusion amount available to the surviving spouse.

The surviving spouse is permitted to be trustee of the credit shelter trust so long as the trust permits it. The risk is that the amount in the credit shelter trust could be included for estate tax purposes in the estate of the surviving spouse when she dies. If the surviving spouse had been treating the credit shelter trust assets as her own money, it will be taxed upon her death. If the trust is carefully drafted and the surviving spouse follows the guidelines, the trust will not be included in the estate of the second spouse to die. Of course, the surviving spouse is not required to be the trustee, and often it is preferable to name an adult child or a bank or trust company as the trustee.

How the Credit Shelter Trust Operates

At the death of the first spouse, a will or living trust does not transfer everything outright to the surviving spouse. Instead, a will or living trust requires that a portion of the estate be transferred into a credit shelter trust. The amount of the estate transferred into the credit shelter trust will be equal to that year's lifetime exclusion amount. Once the credit shelter trust has this amount transferred into it, all other assets that the first spouse owned could be given outright to the surviving spouse.

During the surviving spouse's lifetime, trust income will be distributed to her according to the terms of the trust. The surviving spouse can be entitled to receive all of the income or income distributions may be left to the discretion of the trustee.

Although income may be paid out to the surviving spouse without restriction, the principal must have restrictions on its use if the surviving spouse is the trustee. In that case, distribution of principal must be restricted to an ASCERTAINABLE STANDARD that limits distributions to amounts required for the surviving spouse's health, education, maintenance or support. If the trustee is a bank or trust company, the trust provisions can give broad discretionary powers to the trustee to distribute principal to the surviving spouse.

In addition to receiving income and principal distributions from the trust, the surviving spouse is also permitted to receive an amount equal to the greater of $5,000 or 5% of the value of the trust each year.

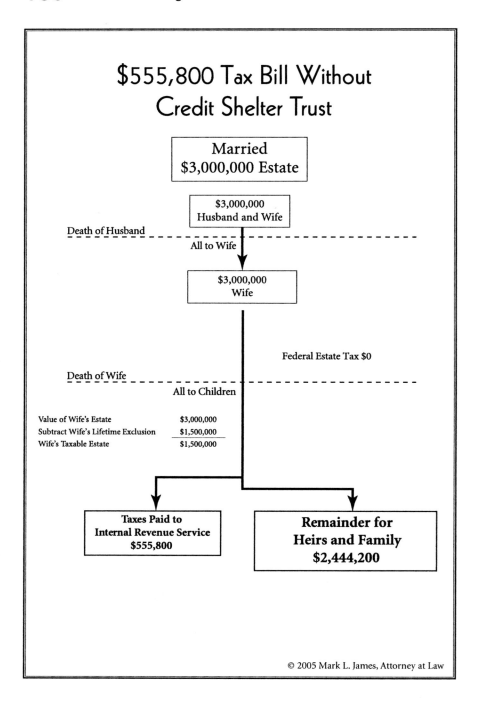

$555,800 Tax Bill Without Credit Shelter Trust

Married
$3,000,000 Estate

$3,000,000
Husband and Wife

Death of Husband

All to Wife

$3,000,000
Wife

Federal Estate Tax $0

Death of Wife

All to Children

Value of Wife's Estate	$3,000,000
Subtract Wife's Lifetime Exclusion	$1,500,000
Wife's Taxable Estate	$1,500,000

Taxes Paid to
Internal Revenue Service
$555,800

Remainder for
Heirs and Family
$2,444,200

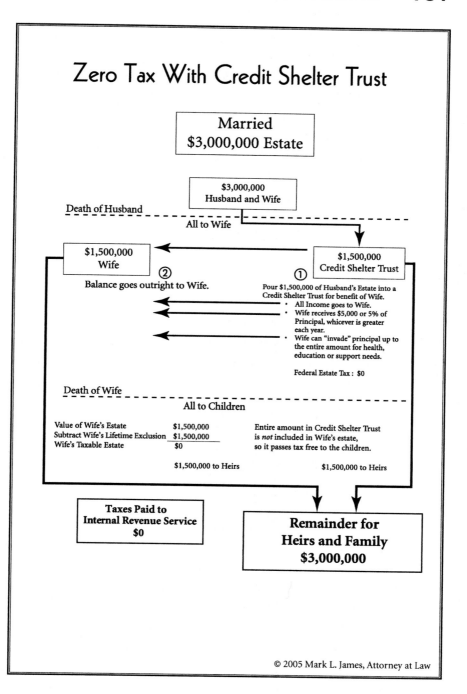

Zero Tax With Credit Shelter Trust

Married
$3,000,000 Estate

$3,000,000
Husband and Wife

Death of Husband
- -
All to Wife

$1,500,000
Wife

②

Balance goes outright to Wife.

$1,500,000
Credit Shelter Trust

①

Pour $1,500,000 of Husband's Estate into a
Credit Shelter Trust for benefit of Wife.
- All Income goes to Wife.
- Wife receives $5,000 or 5% of
  Principal, whicever is greater
  each year.
- Wife can "invade" principal up to
  the entire amount for health,
  education or support needs.

Federal Estate Tax : $0

Death of Wife
- -
All to Children

Value of Wife's Estate	$1,500,000
Subtract Wife's Lifetime Exclusion	$1,500,000
Wife's Taxable Estate	$0

$1,500,000 to Heirs

Entire amount in Credit Shelter Trust
is *not* included in Wife's estate,
so it passes tax free to the children.

$1,500,000 to Heirs

Taxes Paid to
Internal Revenue Service
$0

Remainder for
Heirs and Family
$3,000,000

CALCULATING THE VALUE OF ASSETS NEEDED TO FUND A CREDIT SHELTER TRUST

Since the purpose of the credit shelter trust is to utilize the lifetime exclusion amount of the first spouse to die, married taxpayers whose total estates are less than the $1,500,000 lifetime exclusion amount for 2004 and 2005 do not need a credit shelter trust. For larger estates, however, it becomes necessary to calculate the appropriate portion of the estate that should be used to fund the credit shelter trust of the first spouse to die. The fact that the value of the lifetime exclusion amount is increasing over the course of the next several years makes funding the credit shelter trust particularly challenging. We will now consider two strategies which are used to fund a credit shelter trust.

Mandatory Funding

Mandatory funding refers to the language placed in the will or living trust. When mandatory funding is used, the estate planning documents require the funding of the credit shelter trust. The document directs the executor or trustee to transfer an amount equal to the lifetime exclusion amount into the credit shelter trust. Using the mandatory funding strategy requires that assets be titled correctly during lifetime and the estate planner and client have specifically identified the assets that will fund the credit shelter trust, regardless of which spouse would pass away first.

Caution must be used with mandatory funding because of the increases scheduled in the amount of the lifetime exclusion amount. Estate plans with mandatory funding need to be updated regularly to reflect the changes in the amount. The potential problem is that the first spouse to pass away will have a will or living trust requiring the credit shelter trust to be funded in an amount equal to that year's lifetime exclusion amount, and the credit shelter trust may not even be necessary if the federal estate tax was repealed or if the estate size of both spouses has fallen below the lifetime exclusion amount.

Disclaimer Funding

Another strategy to fund a credit shelter trust is the use of DISCLAIMERS. Disclaiming is more flexible than mandatory funding. For example, if the estate should shrink below the lifetime exclusion amount for any given year, the disclaimer technique would ensure that the credit shelter trust would not be funded, since it would not be necessary.

When using disclaimers to fund the credit shelter trust, the deceased spouse's will or living trust must state that the entire estate is to be paid to the surviving spouse. As a result, the surviving spouse has the option to disclaim any or all of the interest transferred to her from the deceased spouse's estate. Disclaimed assets are transferred into the credit shelter trust instead of being given to the surviving spouse. Since partial disclaimers are permitted, disclaimers are helpful because of the increasing amount of the lifetime exclusion amount. As the value of the lifetime exclusion amount increases, the surviving spouse has the flexibility to direct lesser amounts into the credit shelter trust to save federal estate taxes upon her subsequent death.

Using disclaimer language in your will or living trust also means that if the federal estate tax is repealed, there will be no need to change your will or living trust. This is because disclaimer language transfers everything to your surviving spouse outright, and there would be no need for disclaiming by your surviving spouse to reduce estate taxes.

One disadvantage to disclaimers is the rigid rules concerning disclaiming. The surviving spouse must not "accept any benefit" from the asset to be disclaimed in order to disclaim it. If income is received or other benefits accepted, the assets that generated the income may not be available for disclaimer. For example, if all dividends from stock of the first spouse to die are automatically deposited into a joint checking account and the surviving spouse uses the joint checking account to pay bills, this will have an impact on the ability to disclaim the stock. Another difficulty with disclaimers is that when a spouse dies, she is depending upon the surviving spouse to take action at the appropriate time to voluntarily give up her right to absolute control over the disclaimed assets.

Clayton Q-TIP

A flexible approach to keeping options open is the use of a Clayton Q-TIP trust. The Clayton Q-TIP trust permits the executor of the estate of the deceased spouse to allocate a portion of the estate to the credit shelter trust. The portion allocated to the credit shelter trust is the portion of the Clayton Q-TIP for which the marital deduction is not elected. In effect, the executor calculates the optimum amount to be held in the credit shelter trust to minimize the taxes due when the surviving spouse dies. The executor then elects to have a portion of the deceased spouse's estate equal to that amount transferred to the credit shelter trust. The balance of the decedent's estate will be held in a Q-TIP trust, qualifying for the marital deduction.

This ability to defer the final decision as to the allocation of assets between the marital trust and the credit shelter trust until after the death of the first spouse to die is very flexible. This approach also gives a great deal of authority to the executor. The surviving spouse should not be given the authority to make this determination; it should be exercised by a bank or trust company.

This approach has a number of advantages over the strategy of disclaiming. One advantage is that the rigid requirements for disclaiming are not required to be observed when using a Clayton Q-TIP trust. In addition, a disclaimer must be made within nine months of the date of death. The Q-TIP election can be made up to 15 months after the date of death if the estate files for an extension on the estate tax return.

Strategy Number Three: Make Lifetime Gifts to Family Members

Making gifts to others during your lifetime will lower your federal estate tax because there is no federal estate tax on gifts given during your lifetime. The gift tax has an annual exclusion amount of $11,000. Thus, up to $11,000 of gifts given by you to any single donee in any calendar year is tax free. You and your husband can give a total of $22,000 to each of their children or any other individual. If any single donee receives an amount over $11,000 from one donor, a gift tax return is required, and it would reduce the lifetime exclusion amount to the extent the gift is over $11,000.

The use of this strategy can be illustrated by considering a couple with three children. Since the parents can give $22,000 per year to each child, they would be able to reduce their estate by $66,000 each calendar year. If each of their three children were married, gifts could be made to the spouses of their children also, resulting in gifts of $132,000 given each year to reduce the taxable estate of the parents.

Beware of the Capital Gains Tax on Gifted Assets

Sarah inherited stock from her father back in 1960. At that time, the stock was worth $2 per share. Today, the stock is worth $20 per share. If Sarah gives the stock to her teenage son, Jerry, Jerry's basis in the stock is the same as his mom's, $2 per share. This means that if Jerry decides to sell the stock, he must pay capital gains tax on the difference in value between his mom's basis ($2) and the money Jerry receives for the stock upon its sale.

On the other hand, if Jerry had received his mom's stock as an inheritance from Sarah's estate, the stock would have received a "step-up" in basis. (This means that assets received from the estate of a decedent have a new cost basis equal to the fair market value of the assets on the date of the decedent.) Jerry's basis would be $20 per share (if he inherits the stock). Therefore, if Jerry were to sell the stock for $20 per share after receiving it from his mother's estate, he would pay no capital gains tax.

Gifts to Minors

Giving gifts to minors has a few challenges since one must be at least 18 years old to legally receive a gift. Four options for giving gifts to minors are as follows:

The Uniform Transfer to Minors Act (UTMA)

UTMA provides a simple option for making gifts to minors. Gifts under UTMA are made by transferring the gift to a CUSTODIAN. The custodian is the one responsible to manage the funds in the account for the benefit of the minor. An account may be established for only one minor, and only one person may serve as the custodian. Transfers to the custodian are irrevocable, and the assets are then considered to be owned by the minor, subject to the management authority of the custodian.

For income tax purposes, the minor is considered the owner of the assets and, therefore, income from the assets is reported on the minor's social security number. For estate and gift tax purposes, the custodial account qualifies as a completed gift for purposes of using the $11,000 annual exclusion amount. Parents must keep in mind, however, that if they serve as the custodian of a UTMA account for their children, the value of the custodial account will be included in their estate for federal estate tax purposes.

The custodian has the duty to manage the assets for the benefit of the minor in such fashion as the custodian considers reasonable and necessary. The custodianship ends when the minor reaches age 21, at which time account assets must be given to the minor.

Trusts for Minors

Section 2503(c)

The Internal Revenue Code provides a type of trust for making gifts to minors. Contributions to these trusts qualify for the $11,000 annual exclusion amount as long as the trust meets the following three requirements:

1. Assets transferred to the trust (and any income generated) must be used for the benefit of the minor. These trusts may

have no restrictions on the power of the trustee to use trust assets for the benefit of the minor.

2. Once the minor reaches age 21, whatever is in the trust must be given to the minor.

3. If the minor dies before reaching age 21, the balance of the trust must be paid to his or her estate.

A drawback to the 2503(c) trust is that when the minor reaches age 21, the entire value of the trust must be given to the minor (just like a UTMA account). One strategy to address this is to have a provision in the trust that states that once the minor reaches the age of 21, he or she has a 30-day window of time in which to request that the trust assets be paid to him or her. If the minor makes no request within that window of time, the window then closes and the trust holds the assets until a later time, determined by the trust maker at the time the trust is created, such as age 35 or 40.

The Crummey Trust

The Crummey trust is named after a court case involving a family whose name was Crummey. This type of trust provides that every time a contribution is made to the trust, the trustee is required to notify all beneficiaries of the contribution. The notice gives the trust beneficiaries a limited period of time (30 days for example) within which to instruct the trustee to pay the contribution to them. Any money that the beneficiaries do not withdraw will remain in the trust subject to the terms of the trust. The reason for the window of time for the beneficiaries to withdraw the contribution is so that the contribution to the trust qualifies as a present interest gift. This is important because for gifts to qualify for the donor's $11,000 annual exclusion amount, they must be present interest gifts. This opportunity to withdraw trust contributions is known as a CRUMMEY POWER.

Once the gift is in the trust, it cannot be included in the estate of the one making the gift because of the Crummey withdrawal power given to trust beneficiaries. Unlike other strategies for making gifts to minors, the Crummey trust is not required to pay its trust assets to the minors once they reach age 21. Indeed, the Crummey trust can have provisions that would pay the trust principal to the beneficiary at any age.

One disadvantage of the Crummey trust is the administrative requirement of issuing the Crummey withdrawal letters to the minor's guardian (or directly to the minor once he reaches age 18). The guardian must then notify the trustee whether or not the guardian will take the contribution for the benefit of the minor. Another disadvantage is that the Crummey trust must file its own income tax return each year, as the 2503(c) trust must also do, and pay income tax at the trust income tax rates on any income that is not distributed. Any income distributed to the minor beneficiaries would be taxed at the beneficiary's income tax rate. The Crummey trust is covered in more detail in the section concerning irrevocable life insurance trusts.

Section 529 College Savings Plans

Section 529 was added to the Internal Revenue Code in 1996. This section of the code contains what is formally called a "Qualified Tuition Plan." It is also called a Section 529 Plan or a 529 College Savings Plan. A Section 529 plan is available to all individuals regardless of income or tax bracket. Once contributions have been made to such a plan, the earnings inside the plan will grow tax deferred.

Withdrawals from Section 529 college savings plans are completely free of income tax so long as the withdrawals are used for qualified higher education expenses, which include tuition, books and supplies required by a beneficiary at an eligible educational institution.

Qualified higher education expenses also include reasonable costs incurred by the beneficiary for room and board. An eligible educational institution is restricted to postsecondary educational institutions. Most plans can only be used for undergraduate study at any accredited institution of higher learning within the United States.

What makes Section 529 plans so remarkable is that you (the account owner) can retain control over distributions from the account. Contributions to the plan may only be made in cash. The plan requires a designated beneficiary to be named; you and the beneficiary of the plan are prohibited from directing the investment of the capital in the plan. Your contributions to the plan are revocable, meaning that you can get your money back, but only if you pay the income taxes and a 10% penalty on the earnings. Despite this flexibility, contributions are considered completed gifts, and the amounts deposited in a Section 529 plan are removed from your estate for federal estate tax purposes.

Prior to the creation of Section 529 plans, the federal government did not permit revocable gifts as a way to reduce one's estate. Contributions to 529 plans qualify for the $11,000 annual exclusion amount. In addition, an election is available that permits you to "front end" these plans with as much as $55,000 (representing five years of annual gifts of $11,000). A married couple would be able to start a Section 529 plan with as much as $112,000, while inside the Section 529 plan, income grows tax deferred.

The beneficiary will only get distributions from the plan when you authorize the release of funds. In addition, the beneficiary can be changed at any time to another family member.

In regard to gifting to minors, the Section 529 plan has a number of advantages over the 2503(c) trust. The initial legal and accounting expense for establishing a trust can be avoided by making gifts to a Section 529 plan. In addition, the assets in the 2503(c) trust are required to be distributed to the minor upon reaching age 21. Contributions to a 2503(c) trust are also irrevocable.

The advantages of the 2503(c) trust over the Section 529 plan include the ability of the trustee to actively manage the trust assets. In addition, the assets of the 2503(c) trust can be used for any purpose for the benefit of the minor, not just college education.

In comparison to the UNIFORM TRANSFER TO MINOR'S ACT, the Section 529 plan has a number of advantages. First, the account earnings inside a Section 529 plan grow on a tax-deferred basis, while the UTMA earnings are taxed. In addition, with a Section 529 plan, the beneficiaries can be changed, while this is not possible with the UTMA account. Lastly, the contributor to a Section 529 plan controls the timing of withdrawals. In contrast, when a child reaches age 21, a UTMA account must be closed and distributed to him or her. Section 529 plans are unbeatable if the goal is that the money contributed to the plan is to be used exclusively for college expenses. If you use a Section 529 plan, it is important to state in your will or trust who shall inherit the plan in the event of your death.

Strategy Number Four: Discounting the Value of Assets Remaining in Your Estate

Once the deductions have been fully planned for, the lifetime exclusion amount is protected and assets have been removed and can no longer be included in your taxable estate, the fourth strategy is to discount the value of those assets that remain in your estate. Here, we examine the FAMILY LIMITED PARTNERSHIP. We will also have a brief discussion on the discount that is available for a minority interest in a business.

What Is a Family Limited Partnership?

A family limited partnership (FLP) is a business entity established to segregate and identify specific ownership interests in partnership assets for family members. Once you have carefully considered and maximized the first three strategies, if your heirs would still have federal estate taxes to pay, an FLP then becomes important to consider. Generally, parents are the general partners (maintaining control of the partnership), and the children are the limited partners, receiving only a nominal income interest during the parents' lifetime.

The general partner has full management and control over all partnership assets and determines when and if any money is distributed to the limited partners. The general partner is entitled to a management fee for managing the partnership.

The limited partners have no management authority. The terms of the partnership agreement will limit the transferability of partnership interests so that limited partnership units cannot be bought, sold or transferred without the prior authorization of the general partner.

THE BENEFITS OF A FAMILY LIMITED PARTNERSHIP

The general partner of an FLP controls the partnership. After establishing an FLP, if the parents, as general partners, make gifts to their children of only limited partnership units, the parents can still maintain complete control over the partnership and its assets. They are making gifts to their children that qualify for the $11,000 annual exclusion amount, but maintaining control over all aspects of the underlying assets. The general partner also controls the timing and the amount of distributions of income from the partnership.

An Example of a Limited Family Partnership

Mr. and Mrs. Jones own an eight-unit apartment building worth $500,000. After establishing the Jones Family Limited Partnership, the apartment building is conveyed by deed by Mr. and Mrs. Jones into the name of the Jones Family Limited Partnership.

Mr. and Mrs. Jones now own 100% of the partnership, 2% as general partners and 98% as limited partners. Over the years, the Joneses gift the limited partnership interests to their children, thereby removing a significant portion of the value of the apartment building from their estate. They keep the general partnership interests in order to maintain management control of the partnership.

Another benefit is that the value of limited partnership units that the general partner owns at death can be discounted due to the gifting of limited partnership interests to children during lifetime. This results in lowering the federal estate tax on the partnership interest retained by the one who established the FLP.

A third benefit of FLPs is that the value of gifts of limited partnership interest can be discounted so that a donor can transfer a greater value of assets in a shorter period of time by making gifts of limited partnership units than she could by making gifts of the underlying asset itself.

How Family Limited Partnerships Are Established

A limited partnership agreement is prepared describing in detail the rights and responsibilities of all partners. Typically, a mother and father would hold 2% of the partnership as general partners. They would also initially hold the remaining 98% as limited partners.

After the limited partnership agreement is signed by all partners and a certificate of limited partnership is filed with the state, assets are transferred to the partnership in exchange for both general and limited partnership units.

The assets of the partnership must be valued by a qualified business valuation expert to determine the value of the limited partnership interests. This valuation should be done before assets are transferred into the partnership. The purpose of the valuation is to substantiate the valuation discount that will be claimed on the gifted limited partnership units.

Who Should Consider Using a Family Limited Partnership?

Those who look to transfer assets to the next generation and yet desire to retain control of the assets gifted should consider the FLP. The fact that the FLP shields the assets of the limited partners from creditors is also an advantage.

Maxine's Family Limited Partnership

Maxine owns $110,000 of commercial property and wants to make a gift to her daughter, Sue, which qualifies for the annual exclusion amount. Maxine could convey a one-tenth interest to Sue by deed, which would be an $11,000 gift. Or, Maxine could transfer the property into an FLP and name herself the general partner. Thereafter, Maxine would own 2% of the partnership as a general partner, but maintain 100% control. She would also own the remaining 98% interest in the partnership as a limited partner.

With an FLP, Maxine could gift $11,000 worth of limited partnership units to Sue. This would convey more than a one-tenth interest in the commercial property because limited partnership units are discounted. The value is discounted for two reasons: the minority interest discount, since limited partners have no authority regarding the management of the partnership, and the lack of marketability discount, since a limited partnership agreement restricts the transfer of the limited partnership interests. These two discounts together may total 20% to 40% of the value of the underlying assets.

The following costs should also be taken into account: attorney's fees and accounting fees, the appraisal or valuation fee, updated appraisal fees each time partnership units are given as gifts, the realty transfer tax (if real estate is transferred to the limited partnership) and the cost for the preparation of the partnership's annual income tax return (Form 1065).

Strategy Number Five: Prepay Estate Tax With Discounted Life Insurance Dollars

Life insurance has numerous unique tax benefits in estate planning. With careful planning, life insurance is a useful tool that can pass substantial assets to heirs, totally tax free. Life insurance can be used as an efficient method to replace the value of gifts given to charity. In addition, life insurance may be used to replace the value of an IRA that is given to charity.

Life insurance is also used to provide liquidity to pay federal estate taxes. The fact that federal estate tax is due nine months after death sometimes requires a forced sale of assets to raise the cash needed to pay the tax. Often, stocks and bonds must be sold to raise the cash to pay the tax and the timing of the sale can result in significant losses based on the current price of the stock. If one has life insurance, there will be cash to pay the tax to avoid the forced sale of real estate, a farm or business interest or stocks.

Survivorship life insurance policies insure both spouses on one policy with a last-to-die provision. These policies can be purchased to pay the estate tax for lower premiums than individual policies on each spouse. This policy usually is more likely to be approved, even if one spouse is in poor health, since the death benefit is not paid until the second spouse dies. These policies are sometimes referred to as second-to-die policies.

Life insurance is also used to fund business BUY-SELL AGREEMENTS. Partnerships and closely held businesses should have buy-sell agreements whereby at the death of one partner or shareholder, the surviving partners or shareholders must pay the estate of the deceased for the right to inherit his or her business interests. In order to avoid placing a heavy demand on the cash flow of the business, life insurance is used to fund these agreements to provide the cash necessary to buy out the share of the deceased business owner.

In addition, life insurance is used in business succession planning to provide liquidity for children who are not involved in a family business so they can receive an inheritance other than an interest in the family business.

What Is an Irrevocable Life Insurance Trust?

Life insurance death benefits are exempt from federal income tax. What surprises many, however, is that life insurance death benefits can be included in the estate of the person who owned the policy. For example, if Mother purchased a $500,000 life insurance policy on her life, and she is the owner, at her death the entire $500,000 would be included in her estate for federal estate tax purposes. For this reason, the IRREVOCABLE LIFE INSURANCE TRUST (ILIT) was developed to protect life insurance proceeds from the federal estate tax. These were briefly mentioned earlier when we initially discussed the advantages of trusts generally.

BENEFITS OF AN IRREVOCABLE LIFE INSURANCE TRUST

ILITs will reduce or eliminate federal estate taxes, thereby transferring a greater amount of inheritance to your heirs. This tax benefit is due to the fact that the life insurance in the ILIT is not owned by you. Therefore, since you do not own the policy, upon your death there is no federal estate tax on the death benefits.

ILITs also provide control over the death benefit of life insurance, even after the insured's death. Typically, the beneficiary of life insurance receives the proceeds from the life insurance company immediately after the death of the insured. Beneficiaries have full control over the money as soon as they receive the proceeds. If the insured established an ILIT to receive the insurance benefits, on the other hand, the terms of the ILIT control the proceeds and pay out the distributions over time. One-half of the proceeds could be paid out on the death of the insured, for example, and the remaining one-half could be paid on the fifth annual anniversary of the death of the insured. This type of payout ensures that if the beneficiary squanders the first payout, he or she gets a second chance, five years later, to be a better steward of the money.

HOW LIFE INSURANCE TRUSTS ARE ESTABLISHED

To establish an ILIT, you, the grantor, create the ILIT and name a trustee to administer it. You also name the beneficiaries of the ILIT to receive the proceeds upon your death.

(These are usually the same people named in your will or living trust.) You are not permitted to be the trustee of your own ILIT. Some people name their adult children trustees if they will also be the ultimate beneficiaries of the trust. Banks, trust companies or your CPA can also serve as trustee. The trustee is responsible to obtain the ILIT's taxpayer ID number from the IRS. This is necessary because the ILIT is considered a new taxpayer and is responsible to pay the tax on any income.

The trust must be established before the life insurance is purchased so the trustee can sign the insurance application listing the trust as the applicant, owner and beneficiary of the policy, and you as the insured. If you were to own the policy first, and then transfer it into the trust, the three-year rule would apply. This rule states that if a grantor dies within three years of transferring an existing policy into the trust, the trust will be disregarded and the insurance proceeds become taxable for the estate tax.

OPERATION OF AN IRREVOCABLE LIFE INSURANCE TRUST

Once the ILIT has been designed, written and signed, you fund the ILIT by giving money to the trustee. The trustee then signs the application for life insurance and makes the premium payments to the insurance company. It is important to confirm that you never have any ownership of the life insurance. Therefore, after you establish the ILIT, every contribution you make must be to the trustee, and the trustee then pays the insurance premiums.

Each year, you can gift up to $11,000 to each trust beneficiary into the ILIT. This is the GIFT TAX annual exclusion amount. A husband and wife can gift a total of $22,000 per beneficiary of the ILIT each year.

After the trustee has received a contribution, the trustee must notify each beneficiary that a contribution has been made to the trust. The reason for this notice is that the gift must be a PRESENT INTEREST in order to qualify for the gift tax annual exclusion of up to $11,000 per year. Each contribution to the trust is considered a gift to the beneficiaries. Each beneficiary must be given reasonable notice (30 days) to claim his portion of the gift. If a beneficiary does not claim his or her portion of the contribution, the trustee is then free to invest it wherever the trustee desires, which would be to pay insurance premiums. Since the long-term benefit of tax-free life insurance proceeds is more substantial than the short-term gift to the trust, a beneficiary may waive the right of withdrawal offered in the Crummey letter. After any beneficiaries decline to demand distribution of their proportionate share of the gift from the trust, the trustee then uses the gifted money to pay the life insurance premium.

You must be cautious if you transfer existing life insurance policies into your life insurance trust. If you die within three years of the date of transferring an existing policy into a trust, the IRS will include the total death benefit in your taxable estate. Transferring existing policies into a life insurance trust may also trigger the gift tax.

The Bob and Shirley Jones Irrevocable Life Insurance Trust

Mr. and Mrs. Jones established the Bob and Shirley Jones Irrevocable Life Insurance Trust naming their son, Tim, the trustee. The contributions that the Joneses make to the ILIT are in the form of a check made out to Tim Jones, trustee of the Bob and Shirley Jones Irrevocable Life Insurance Trust. After the grantors give the check to the trustee, the trustee deposits the check into a noninterest-bearing checking account. Since the trust has its own taxpayer ID number, any interest earned is taxed to the trust. By using a noninterest-bearing checking account, there is no taxable income, and the trust can avoid the expense of filing tax returns.

What Happens When the Grantor Dies?

Upon the death of the grantor, the trustee collects the life insurance proceeds and distributes the ILIT assets as instructed in the trust document. The trustee must not directly pay the expenses or taxes due on the estate of the grantor. Although the trustee has access to this tax-free liquid fund to pay taxes and final expenses, if she used this money to pay the taxes or last expenses of the deceased grantor directly from the ILIT, then the entire amount in the ILIT would be taxed for federal estate tax purposes. Therefore, ILIT cash must be either loaned to the estate or used to purchase assets from the estate in order to use it to pay estate bills and taxes.

Tim and Jim Receive Crummey Letters

Mr. and Mrs. Jones named their two children, Tim and Jim, as the beneficiaries of their ILIT. Since Mr. and Mrs. Jones can each give $11,000 to each son, they can contribute a total amount of $44,000 to the insurance trust free of gift tax considerations. Once the $44,000 has been received by Tim, as trustee, he is required to send a letter to his brother. (Since Tim is the trustee, he is deemed to have knowledge of the gift and is not required to receive notice of trust contributions.) The letter tells Jim that: (a) a $44,000 gift has been made to the trust; (b) Jim's proportionate share of the gift is $22,000; and, (c) Jim has 30 days within which to notify the trustee to distribute this amount to him. These letters of notification are called "Crummey letters." These letters are described in more detail in the preceding section on gifts to minors.

"CAN'T I JUST HAVE MY CHILDREN OWN THE POLICY?"

After reviewing the requirements of ILITs, many people reach the conclusion that it would be simpler to have their adult children own the life insurance policy. If adult children own the policy, there is no requirement to go through the steps needed with ILITs. The life insurance will still be tax free at the death of the grantor because the grantor does not own

Irrevocable Life Insurance Trust Procedures

Task	To Be Completed By	Required Completion Date
Design and write trust	Attorney	Before life insurance application is signed
Obtain tax ID number from the IRS	Attorney	When trust is written
Sign trust agreement	Trustee and Grantors	
Prepare application for life insurance	Insurance agent	After trust is written and signed
Trustee signs application as owner and names trust the beneficiary	Trustee	After trust and life insurance applications are completed
Open a no-interest checking account in trust's tax ID number to deposit trust contributions and pay insurance premiums	Trustee	Immediately after signing trust
Grantor makes check out to trustee	Grantor	
Trustee endorses all checks and deposits them into trust checking account	Trustee	
Send Crummey withdrawal notices to beneficiaries	Trustee	As soon as funds are contributed to trust
Pay the insurance premium after the withdrawal period has passed by writing checks to the insurance company out of the trust checking account	Trustee	After Crummey withdrawal period has passed
Contribute additional funds to trust to pay premium in future years	Grantor	At least 30 days before premium is due
Upon death of insureds, distribution of trust assets	Trustee	According to the terms of the trust

the policy, the grantor's children do. Although it may appear simpler to have adult children own the life insurance, there are a number of risks to be considered:

- Loss of Control: As owners of the policy, the children have the power to change the beneficiary. In addition, they would be free to either cancel the policy or withdraw all the cash value from the policy, reducing the death benefit.

- Your Children May Not Use the Death Benefit as Planned: As owners of the policy, children receive all the proceeds directly from the insurance company. Your plan might be for them to use this money to pay last expenses and federal estate taxes, but there is no requirement for them to do so. They may use the life insurance proceeds to do as they please. In addition, you would be giving the money to pay the insurance premiums directly to your children and hope that the children would then use it to pay the insurance premiums.

- The Policy Would Be Subject to the Children's Creditors: The cash value of the policy is available to the creditors of each child in the event of bankruptcy, a business failure, high medical bills or a divorce.

- If Son or Daughter Dies First, Their Surviving Spouse Would Own the Policy: If the surviving son-in-law or daughter-in-law should remarry, the new husband or wife would be an owner. The cash value is included in the estate of the child if he or she dies before the parents.

- Administrative Difficulties: If the policy is owned jointly by children, then all the children must sign all necessary forms.

Disadvantages of Irrevocable Life Insurance Trusts

There are two disadvantages to irrevocable life insurance trusts:

1. ILITs cannot be amended or revoked once established. The grantor can stop making the contributions that the trustee

was using to pay premiums, but that does not terminate the ILIT. The ILIT would continue to own the remaining cash value in the life insurance policy.

2. The grantor loses the use of the money contributed. In addition, the grantor will not have access to any growth in the cash value. If the federal estate tax is repealed, and the ILIT was established for the sole purpose of avoiding the federal estate tax, the grantor may not want to have a high cash value locked up in the ILIT.

WHO SHOULD CONSIDER USING AN IRREVOCABLE LIFE INSURANCE TRUST?

Those who have significant estate tax exposure should give these trusts serious consideration. In addition, those who wish to have continued control over the disposition of life insurance benefits even after their death should consider an ILIT.

Summary

Although the federal estate tax has a rate as high as 48% on estates over $1,500,000 (in 2004), we have seen five fundamental strategies that can be used to minimize the effects of this tax. More planning opportunities are available to those who are married, although single taxpayers have a number of planning strategies as well.

Step 9

Enjoy Peace of Mind

*Y*OU'VE DONE IT! You have walked through the steps of estate planning. Take a deep breath and enjoy the peace of mind.

You used to think that estate planning was just too difficult to understand and that as a woman you had too much else to think about to pursue estate planning. Now you realize that you have too much to lose to not plan your estate. And now you are empowered to do your estate planning carefully, thoughtfully and with foresight. You understand how to protect yourself as you move through the seasons of life, and you know how to benefit those you love.

It is up to you now to do it — to establish and implement your estate plan. Start today by establishing your estate planning team. Call your attorney, accountant and investment advisor before this day is over. Make the appropriate appointments. Have confidence in yourself — you understand the estate planning fundamentals now. You are indeed fully prepared to tackle the questions you will be asked and the decisions you must make.

As a young single woman, you know that you want to start thinking about retirement now. Planning now will make your years of marriage and children later so much more joyful and stress free. Having an estate plan now is a strong signal that you understand what you want out of life. Whether you marry or not, it makes you all the more prepared to care for yourself and others whom you care about and love.

As a married woman, you realize that you may very well outlive your husband. You have learned how to stay in control of your assets as you move through the seasons of your life. You also know how to control the distribution of your assets after your death to benefit those you love. If you divorce or remarry, you also understand that there are special considerations you need to make under those circumstances to protect yourself and to protect your loved ones.

As a widow, you are at a critical time to make these decisions. It is never too late to plan. And you will never regret later the thoughtfulness you put into your estate plan now.

Summary of Steps to Successful Estate Planning:

1. Remember that as a woman you are very unique.

2. Find your estate planning advisor and assemble your estate planning team.

3. Learn the laws of your state regarding estate planning tools.

4. Stay in control of your assets as you move through the seasons of life.

5. Stay in control of your assets and their distribution in the event of death, divorce, remarriage or widowhood.

6. Make the world a better place with charitable giving.

7. Don't forget to include retirement plans, IRAs and 401(k)s in your estate plan.

8. Determine the best way to pay zero estate tax.

9. Enjoy the peace of mind you have as a result of successful estate planning.

You have the knowledge now to be thoughtful, to consider leaving a legacy to that charity you've worked hard for all your life. You understand so much about trusts that you can plan intelligently with your estate planning team, fully participating in decisions about your life, rather than just going along with what experts tell you. You also understand retirement plans, IRAs and 401(k)s and can see with foresight now how they all fit together into your global life plan. What a relief to have clarity in this otherwise foggy area of life management.

Finally, all that tax legislation should be a bit clearer now, enough so that you can know when you will be vulnerable to estate and inheritance taxes. Of course you don't know everything, but you do know enough to get your team started in the direction you want to take your life and your estate plan.

So have you been sitting in an airport somewhere reading this book while you are traveling to be with those you love? We'll bet you are a lot like the woman at the beginning of this book. Most likely, you have given a good portion of your life to those you love. That's just what women do. Now you know, however, that those times with those you love will be much more wonderful if you take care of yourself with proper planning now.

Summary

Women need peace of mind, comprehensive thinking and minimal stress in the process of estate planning. Following the steps set out in this book allows you the freedom to gain each of these. You have the knowledge now to be thoughtful about your plans, for yourself and those you love. You are free and prepared to consider leaving a legacy of your lifetime. Foresight, clarity and peace of mind are yours, and the work you do now will benefit those you love forever.

About the Authors

*L*ynne Marie Kohm is the John Brown McCarty Professor of Family Law at Regent University's School of Law. She earned her law degree from Syracuse College of Law and graduated with a Bachelor of Arts degree in philosophy from Albany University. Professor Kohm has published prolifically on legal areas of concern to women, children and families. She teaches family law; wills, trusts and estates; elder law; bioethics; gender and the law; and human life and death. She teaches law students and lawyers many of the legal concepts and techniques that assist individuals and families in planning for incapacity and estate distribution.

Prior to teaching, Professor Kohm practiced law in New York, concentrating in the areas of estate planning, probate administration, real estate and family law. She is licensed to practice law in Virginia, New York, Florida, Massachusetts and the District of Colombia. She is also a certified guardian ad litem. Her professional affiliations include the Virginia State Bar Family Law Section Board of Governors, the American Bar Association, the Christian Legal Society, the Alliance Defense Fund, the Eagle Forum, Concerned Women for America and Bethany Christian Services. She lectures to public forums on various aspects of estate planning in numerous jurisdictions.

Special acknowledgments must be given to several individuals. Deep gratitude and appreciation is extended to Shawn Marie Holland, Lori Diane Osgood and Robert P. Stenzhorn, C.P.A., M.B.A., for their invaluable research, insight, suggestions and editing skills. Each made priceless contributions to this book.

Professor Kohm may be contacted at:

Regent University School of Law
1000 Regent University Drive
Virginia Beach, VA 23464
(757) 226-4335

The author of three books about estate planning, Mark L. James, M.B.A., J.D., LL.M. (tax), is an of counsel attorney with Hartman, Underhill and Brubaker LLP, a Lancaster County, Pa., law firm. He is a graduate of

Grove City College where he received his B.A. He received his M.B.A. from Michigan State University. His law degree was earned from the Regent University School of Law in Virginia Beach, Va. (where he currently serves as a member of the board of trustees). He continued his law studies at the College of William and Mary, Marshall-Wythe School of Law, graduating with a Master of Laws in Taxation (LL.M.). Prior to law school, Mr. James was a financial advisor with a Wall Street brokerage firm. He has also served as a planned giving representative with an international nonprofit organization where he raised millions of dollars in deferred gifts using charitable estate planning strategies. His law practice is concentrated in the areas of estate planning, estate and trust administration and business law.

Mr. James' professional affiliations include membership in the National Academy of Elder Law Attorneys, the National Association of Estate Planners and Councils and the National Committee on Planned Giving. Mr. James lectures frequently on subjects within his area of expertise for a variety of professional and civic organizations including financial and estate planning professionals, nonprofit organizations, colleges and retirement communities.

Mr. James can be contacted by writing:

Barron Publishing Co.
Post Office Box 532
State College, PA 16804
e-mail: markj@barronpublishing.com

Appendices

The Estate Planning Questionnaire

Family Information
Client

NAME _____

BIRTH DATE _____ SOCIAL SECURITY NO. _____

HOME ADDRESS _____

CITY _____ STATE _____ ZIP _____

TOWNSHIP/BOROUGH/COU_____

TELEPHONE NO. (_____) _____

PLACE OF BIRTH _____ CITIZENSHIP _____

PREVIOUSLY MARRIED? _____

HOW TERMINATED _____ TERMINATION DATE _____

OCCUPATION _____ EMPLOYER _____

BUSINESS ADDRESS _____

CITY _____ STATE _____ ZIP _____

BUSINESS TELEPHONE NO. (_____) _____

Spouse (if applicable)

NAME _____

BIRTH DATE _____ SOCIAL SECURITY NO. _____

HOME ADDRESS _____

CITY _____ STATE _____ ZIP _____

TOWNSHIP/BOROUGH/COUNTY _____

TELEPHONE NO. (_____) _____

PLACE OF BIRTH _____ CITIZENSHIP _____

PREVIOUSLY MARRIED? _____

HOW TERMINATED _____ TERMINATION DATE _____

OCCUPATION _____ EMPLOYER _____

BUSINESS ADDRESS _____

CITY _____ STATE _____ ZIP _____

BUSINESS TELEPHONE NO. (_____) _____

Profile of Your Children

Name of Child	From Which Marriage*	Age	Residence: Street, City, State & Zip	Marital Status	Number of Children For Child

* Use: Y = Child of this marriage   H = Husband's previous marriage   W = Wife's previous marriage

Current Estate Profile

	Yes	No
1. Does any family member have significant long-term health problems or other special needs?		
2. Do you now (or do you expect to) support anyone other than a child, such as a parent?		
3. Have you lived in any states other than your current state during your marriage?		
4. Do you and your spouse have a pre-nuptial agreement?		
5. Do you (or your spouse) expect a significant inheritance?		
6. Have you (or your spouse) created any trusts?		
7. Are you (or your spouse) a beneficiary of any trusts?		
8. Have you (or your spouse) ever filed a federal gift tax return?		
9. Do you (and your spouse) have a durable power of attorney?		
10. Do you (and your spouse) have a will or living trust?		
11. Do you (and your spouse) have a living will?		
12. Would you like to discuss a gift program to your children, or a trust for their benefit?		
13. Do you have any assets located in other states?		

Estate Asset Summary

	Asset	Client Owns	Spouse Owns	Jointly Owned
A.	Cash, Bank Accounts, Money Market Funds & CDs	$	$	$
B.	Money Owed to You			
C.	Bonds, Bond Funds & Treasury Bills			
D.	Stocks and Mutual Funds			
E.	Personal Residence (Today's Market Value)			
F.	Second Home (Today's Market Value)			
G.	Total of Other Real Estate (Today's Market Value)			
H.	Closely-Held Business Interests and/or Farm			
I.	Retirement Plans (including IRAs)			
J.	Interests in Estates and Trusts			
K.	Life Insurance (Face Value)			
L.	Automobiles			
M.	Household Furnishings & Personal Assets			
N.	Other Assets (such as Annuities)			
	Totals			

Please use your best estimate of these values in the applicable column.

Liabilities

Who Owes?*	To Whom Owed	Nature of Debt**	Current Balance

*Use: H = Husband   W = Wife   JT = Joint   **Such as Bills, Mortgages, Notes Payable, etc.*

Distribution of Your Assets | Yes | No

1.	If Husband dies before Wife, 100% of estate to go to Wife?		
2.	If Wife dies before Husband, 100% of estate to go to Husband?		
3.	If Husband and Wife are both deceased, 100% of estate to go to all children equally?		

4. If any of the above answers are "No," list the names of your children, church, charity or others and the percentage (%) of your estate you desire to give to each. Alternatively, note the specific amount of cash or other assets you want to give to certain people or charities.

        Name   Percentage

1. _____

2. _____

3. _____

5. If you and your spouse die prematurely, at what age do you want your children (or your grandchildren if both of their parents die prematurely) to receive your estate? Until this age, the trustee will take care of their financial needs. If no age is specified, they will receive 100% at age 18.

_____% at age _____   _____% at age _____   Balance at age _____

6. If one of your children dies before you, that child's share to go to:

    1. ___ His/Her Children   2. ___ Your Other Living Children

             3. ___ Your Deceased Child's Spouse

7. If none of your descendants are living at the time of your death, who do you want to receive your assets, such as extended family, friends or charities? Please list amounts and/or percentages.

        Name   Percentage

1. _____

2. _____

3. _____

List in order of preference persons or institutions (such as banks or trust companies) you wish for executor. Name at least two if you do not name a bank. Husband is usually named first for Wife, and Wife is usually named first for Husband, and each would then name someone else as an Alternate.

As Husband, I desire to name my wife as my executor. _____ Yes _____ No

As Wife, I desire to name my husband as my executor. _____ Yes _____ No

How should Executors #1 and #2 serve? ☐ Jointly ☐ First #1, Then #2

Executor of Your Estate

	Name	Relationship	Address	City, State & Zip
1.				
2.				

If any of your children are under 18, indicate first and second choices for guardians for them if something should happen to the two of you. (Name two – a first choice and an Alternate.)

Guardians for Your Minor Children

	Name	Relationship	Address	City, State & Zip
1.				
2.				

List in order of preference persons or banks you wish to be trustee for minor children or others. (If you do not name a bank, please name at least two choices – a first choice and an Alternate.)

How should Executors #1 and #2 serve? ☐ Jointly ☐ First #1, Then #2

Trustee of Trusts That You Create in Your Will

	Name	Relationship	Address	City, State & Zip
1.				
2.				

You will be the initial trustee(s) unless you designate otherwise. At your death or disability, your successor trustee (adult children, financial advisor, trusted friend, bank, or a trust company) will manage your trust. Name more than one individual in case your first is unable to serve.

Who Will Manage Your Revocable Living Trust?

	Name	Relationship	Address	City, State & Zip
1.				
2.				

The Professional Designations of Estate Planning Advisors

The following is a brief description of the professional and academic qualifications of estate planning advisors and a note about the organization that confers the designation.

AEP - Accredited Estate Planner. A professional designation awarded by the National Association of Estate Planners and Councils. This designation is for estate planning practitioners who complete examination requirements and meet continuing education requirements. There are about 1200 members who hold this designation. The National Association of Estate Planners & Councils can be contacted at 270 S. Bryn Mawr Avenue, Bryn Mawr, PA 19010-2195, phone 610-526-1389, website - www.naepc.org.

CELA - Certified Elder Law Attorney. Attorneys with a CELA designation have been certified as an elder law attorney by The National Elder Law Foundation (NELF). To achieve this certification the Elder Law attorney must practice for at least five years and have an in-depth knowledge of the legal issues that impact the elderly. The NELF Certification process is approved by the American Bar Association and requires the attorney to complete a comprehensive examination. The National Elder Law Foundation can be contacted at 1604 North Country Club Road, Tucson, AZ 85716. Phone 520-881-1076, website - webmaster@nelf.org

CFP - Certified Financial Planner. The individual holding this designation has completed the Certified Financial Board of Standards academic certification requirements. More then 36,000 individuals use the CFP certification mark. Certified Financial Planner Board of Standards can be contacted at 1700 Broadway, Suite 2100, Denver, CO, 80290-2101. Phone 303-830-7500, website - www.CPF-Board.org

CFRE - Certified Fund Raising Executive. This designation is conferred on qualifying fund-raising executives after five years of experience. It requires an application and a written examination. The CFRE Program is governed by the CFRE Professional Certification Board. The Program and the Board are administered in cooperation with a number of leading philanthropic associations.

CFS - Certified Fund Specialist. This designation is awarded to those who have completed a study course and examination. More than 10,000 people have this designation awarded by the Institute of Business and Finance. The Institute of Business and Finance can be contacted at 7911 Herschel Ave., Suite 201, La Jolla, CA 92037-4413. Phone 800-848-2029, website - www.icfs.com

CFSC - Certified Financial Services Counselor. This designation is obtained through attending the American Banker's Association's (ABA) National Graduate Trust School (Northwest University) in Illinois. Contact the American Banker's Association at 1120 Connecticut Avenue, NW, Washington, DC 20036. Phone 800-338-0626, website - www.aba.com

ChFC - Chartered Financial Consultant. One holding this designation has completed an educational program offered by the American College. In addition to examinations, the holder of this designation must meet experience and ethical standards and complete continuing education courses. Over 32,000 professional advisors have received this designation. The American College can be contacted at 270 S. Bryn Mawr Avenue, Bryn Mawr, PA 19010. Phone 610-526-1000, website - www.amercoll.edu .

CLU - Chartered Life Underwriter. A designation conferred upon those who have completed an educational program offered by the American College. This individual has also met experience and ethical standards and is required to complete continuing education. Approximately 85,000 have received the CLU designation. See Chartered Financial Consultant for contact information at the American College.

CPA - Certified Public Accountant. This individual has met academic qualifications such as Bachelors or Masters degree in accounting and has passed a series of state certifying examinations and meets experience qualifications in the area of public accounting.

CPA/PFS - Personal Financial Specialist. About 2500 CPAs have acquired this designation. Those holding the PFS designation must be existing CPAs who have experience in financial planning and pass an examination. The CPA/PFS is awarded by the American Institute of Certified Public Accountants. AICPA can be contacted at American Institute of Certified Public Accountants, Personal Financial Planning Division, 1211 Avenue of the Americas, New York, NY, 10036-8775. Phone 888-777-7077, website - www.aicpa.org

CSA - Certified Senior Advisor. The Society of Certified Senior Advisors grants the Certified Senior Advisor designation. It is an educational organization that provides training on senior issues to professionals who work with seniors. There are over 3,000 holding this designation who are required to complete continuing education. The Society of Certified Senior Advisors can be contacted at 1777 South Bellaire Street, Suite 230, Denver, CO 80222. Phone 1-800-653-1785, website - www.society-csa.com.

CTFA - Certified Trust and Financial Advisor. The American Institute of Banking awards this designation to those who meet educational requirements and pass extensive examinations in the areas of tax law, investments, personal finance and fiduciary responsibilities. The American Institute of Banking can be contacted at 80 Maiden Lane, New York City, NY, 10036. Phone 212-480-3200, website - www.aibny.edu

EA - Enrolled Agent. A designation given by the Internal Revenue Service to enable individuals to represent others before the IRS.

ESQ - Esquire. This is a popular designation given to licensed attorneys who are actively engaged in the practice of law.

FIC - Fraternal Insurance Counselor. This designation is conferred by the Fraternal Field Managers' Association on those who successfully complete educational requirements and meet required qualifications. Contact the National Fraternal Congress of America at 1240 Iroquois Drive - Suite 300, Naperville, IL 60563. Website - www.nfcanet.org.

J.D. - Juris Doctor. The academic degree awarded to one who has completed a three-year study of law. The initials J.D. are usually used instead of the letters ESQ." to designate an attorney who has graduated from law school but who is not actively engaged in the practice of law.

LL.M. (tax) - Master of Laws in Taxation. An academic degree awarded to attorneys who have completed law school and have, in addition, completed further academic work at a law school to achieve a second law degree with a concentration in tax law.

LUTCF - Life Underwriter Training Council Fellow. This designation is awarded to persons in the life insurance industry who have completed courses relating to life and health insurance. The designation is conferred by the Life Underwriter Training Council. There are currently about 60,000 persons who have completed this program. Life Underwriting Training Council can be contacted at 7625 Wisconsin Avenue, Bethesda, MD 20814-3560. Phone 301-913-5882, website - www.lutc.org.

MBA - Master of Business Administration. An academic degree awarded to those who have completed a four-year undergraduate degree program and have continued on with further academic studies concentrated in areas related to business administration.

MT - Master of Taxation. An academic degree conferred upon those who have completed a four- year college degree and have continued on to post-graduate studies specializing in the area of taxation.

Glossary

AB Trust - A trust giving a surviving spouse a lifetime interest in assets of a deceased spouse. This trust is designed to save on estate taxes by giving a surviving spouse only the income from the assets of the first spouse to die. Also known as a credit shelter trust" or bypass trust."

Abatement - A reduction in the amount of a bequest under a will because the assets of the estate are insufficient to pay all debts, taxes, and bequests in full.

Ademption - The failure of a specific bequest of assets to be made, because the decedent did not own the assets at the time of death.

Adjusted Gross Estate - For federal estate tax purposes, the gross estate less debts, administration expenses, and losses during administration.

Administration - The process of settling a decedent's estate. The duties include valuing estate assets, filing tax returns and paying taxes, and distributing assets to heirs.

Administration Expenses - The expenses incurred during the administration of an estate. These include legal and accounting fees, appraisal fees, and distribution costs.

Administrator - Person or institution appointed by a court to represent an estate when there is no will. Also called a personal representative.

Advance Medical Directive - See Living Will."

Advancement - A bequest made in a will, which is reduced because of gifts made to that person during lifetime.

Affidavit - A written statement made under oath before a notary public or authorized officer of the court.

Agent - The person given authority by one signing a power of attorney to transact business in his or her name.

Alternate Beneficiary - The person or organization named to receive assets if the primary beneficiary dies before the one naming the beneficiaries.

Alternate Valuation Date - The date six months after a decedent's death for federal estate tax purposes. The personal representative has the option of valuing estate assets as of the date of death or the alternate valuation date, if certain criteria are met.

Anatomical Gift - A gift of one or more body organs upon death.

Ancillary Administration - Administration of an estate in another state in addition to the state where the decedent lived. Typically required when the decedent owns real estate in another state.

Annual Exclusion Amount - The amount ($11,000 adjusted for inflation) one is permitted to give away to any other person each year without paying gift tax or filing a gift tax return. There is no limit on the number of people to whom gifts can be made each calendar year.

Annuity - A contractual right to receive a fixed sum of money at specific intervals either for life or for a minimum term of years.

Annuity Trust - One form of charitable remainder trust that pays a fixed amount to a person regularly. The amount paid is based on the value of a gift at the time the trust is established, age of donor, and interest rates.

Applicable Credit Amount - See Lifetime Exclusion Amount."

Ascertainable Standard - The right of a surviving spouse serving as the trustee, to invade a credit shelter trust, without causing the trust's assets to be included in his or her estate. The power is limited to using trust assets for the spouse's health, education, maintenance, and support."

Bargain Sale - The sale of assets for less than their current fair market value.

Basis - The amount paid to acquire an asset. The value is used to determine gain or loss for income tax purposes upon the asset's subsequent sale.

Beneficiary - The person or organization that receives assets from a will or trust after the death of the trust grantor. The word also refers to those who receive assets from an annuity, life insurance policy, or retirement plan.

Bequest - A gift left to a person or organization under a will or trust.

Buy-Sell Agreement - A contract between partners or shareholders of a corporation that determines the conditions and price for a buyout by one at the death or retirement of the other.

Bypass Trust - A trust for married couples that does not qualify for the unlimited estate tax marital deduction. Commonly referred to as the family trust, or B trust, or credit shelter trust. It is designed to use the lifetime exclusion amount of the first spouse to die.

Capital Gains Tax - Income tax on the gain from the sale of an asset. The amount taxed is calculated by subtracting tax basis from the sale price.

Certificate of Trust - A brief version of a trust that verifies the trust's existence, describes trustee's powers, and identifies the successor trustee.

Charitable Lead Trust - A trust in which a charity receives income for a certain period of time with the remainder passing to the donor's beneficiaries after a specified period of time.

Charitable Remainder Trust - A trust where the beneficiary receives income payments for lifetime or a term of years (not to exceed 20). Upon the beneficiary's death, assets remaining in the trust pass to a charitable organization.

Co-Trustees - Two or more individuals appointed to serve together to manage a trust's assets. A corporate trustee can also be a co-trustee.

Codicil - A legal document which changes or modifies the will.

Community Property States - States in which all assets acquired by either partner in a marriage are considered owned one half by each partner. Community property states are Arizona, California, Idaho, Louisiana, Nevada, New Mexico, Texas, Washington, and Wisconsin.

Conservation Easement - A permanent easement placed on real estate that prevents it from being developed into commercial real estate.

Contest of a Will - Legal action taken to change or prevent the distribution of assets as set forth in a decedent's will. The usual claims are that the decedent was incompetent when they signed their will or they were under the undue influence of another person.

Contingent Beneficiary - An alternate person or organization selected in case the primary beneficiary dies before the one naming beneficiaries.

Corporate Trustee - A bank trust department or trust company that specializes in managing trusts.

Corpus - Assets the grantor places in trust. Also known as the principal of a trust.

Credit Shelter Trust - A trust established under a will or living trust to take advantage of the lifetime exclusion amount of the first spouse to die. (Also known as a bypass trust or a B trust)

Crummey Power - The right held by the beneficiary of a trust to withdraw from the trust a portion of every contribution to the trust.

Custodian - The person named to manage a minor's assets under the Uniform Transfer to Minors Act.

Decedent - A person who has died.

Deed - A legal document by which one person transfers title to real estate to another person or persons.

Disclaimer - The refusal to accept assets one is entitled to receive. The disclaimed assets will be transferred to the next person as provided by a will or trust. Disclaimers must be completed within nine months of death.

Domicile - The state in which one has their permanent residence.

Donee - A person who receives a gift.

Donor - A person who makes a gift.

Durable Power of Attorney - A power of attorney which continues as a legal document even if the principal later becomes incapacitated.

Durable Power of Attorney for Health Care - A legal document that gives someone the authority to make health care decisions for the principal in the event he or she is unable to make them.

Elective Share - A portion of the estate that a surviving spouse is entitled to by law regardless of what the decedent's will states.

Escheat - Assets that go to a state government because there are no legal heirs to claim it.

Estate - Assets or property that one owns or has the rights to possess.

Estate Administration - The process of handling the affairs of decedent's estate.

Estate Planning - The process of developing a plan to provide for the tax effective and orderly distribution of an individual's assets at the time of death, or the management of their assets during lifetime if they become incapacitated.

Estate Tax - A tax imposed by the federal government on the right of a person to transfer assets at death. This transfer tax is applicable to estates valued over and above the lifetime exclusion amount" which is $1,500,000 for 2004.

Executor - The person or institution appointed in a will to administer the estate, deal with the probate court, collect assets and distribute them as specified. Also known as the personal representative.

Fair Market Value - The value at which assets are included in the gross estate for federal estate tax purposes. The price at which assets would change hands between a willing buyer and a willing seller.

Family Limited Partnership - A type of partnership that provides asset protection and allows for management and control of assets by the general partners.

Fiduciary - A person or institution in a position of trust and responsibility. Examples are the executor of a will, trustee of a trust, or agent under a power of attorney.

Five and Five Powers - The right of a trust beneficiary to withdraw from the principal of a trust the greater of 5% of the value of the trust or $5,000 per year.

Funding a Trust - The process of transferring assets into a trust.

Generation-Skipping Transfer (GST) Tax - A tax assessed on gifts in excess of $1,060,000 (adjusted for inflation) to grandchildren, great-grandchildren, and others at least two generations below the individual making the gift.

Gift Tax - A federal tax imposed on gifts made while living. $11,000 (adjusted for inflation) per person per year is exempt from gift tax. See annual exclusion amount."

Grantor - The person who establishes a trust. Also called the settlor or trustor.

Grantor Trust - A trust where income is taxable to the grantor because he or she retains substantial control over the trust assets or retains certain administrative powers. All trust values are included in grantor's estate for estate and inheritance tax purposes.

Gross Estate - The total value of assets left by the decedent. The amount required to be included in his or her estate for estate tax purposes.

Guardian - A person appointed by the court to have custody over the person or the assets (or both) of a minor or incapacitated person.

Guardian of the Estate - An individual or institution appointed by the court to manage the assets of a minor or an incapacitated person.

Guardian of the Person - An individual or institution appointed by the court to care for a minor or an incapacitated person.

Heir - One who receives the assets of a decedent by operation of law or by will or trust.

Holographic Will - A will that is completely handwritten.

Incapacity - The mental state of being unable to make decisions regarding management of one's own assets or medical needs.

Inheritance Tax - A tax on the heir of a decedent for assets inherited. Tax rates depend on the relationship of the heir to the decedent.

Inter Vivos Trust - A trust established during one's lifetime. Also called a living trust.

Intestacy Laws - State laws which control who will receive the assets of a person who dies without a will.

Intestate - A person who dies without a will; that person is said to have died intestate.

Irrevocable Trust - A trust that cannot be revoked, canceled or amended once it is established. The opposite of a revocable trust.

Issue - Direct descendants of an individual such as children, grandchildren and great-grandchildren.

Joint Ownership - Two or more persons owning the same asset.

Joint Tenants with Right of Survivorship - One way to take title to jointly owned assets. At the death of one joint owner, the surviving joint owner(s) automatically receive the deceased person's interest. (See also tenants in common" and tenants by the entirety.")

Lapse - The failure of a bequest in a will that occurs when the intended recipient dies before the testator.

Letters Testamentary - The document issued by the court authorizing the executor to discharge his responsibilities.

Life Estate - The right to use assets and receive income from them during one's lifetime. At death, that person's rights terminate.

Lifetime Exclusion Amount - The dollar value of assets that one can give to a non-spouse either during lifetime or at death free of estate taxes. For 2002, the dollar value is $1 million.

Limited Power of Attorney - A power of attorney that limits the agent's authority to certain actions.

Living Trust - A trust established by a person during his or her lifetime. If it is revocable, it can be amended or terminated anytime. The trust becomes irrevocable upon death.

Living Will - A document that states a person's wishes regarding certain types of medical treatment in the event of a terminal illness or coma.

Marital Deduction - A federal estate tax deduction for assets received by the deceased's spouse. Amount is unlimited if the surviving spouse is a U.S. citizen.

Marital Trust - A trust consisting of assets qualifying for the federal estate tax marital deduction.

Medicaid - Program funded by the federal and state government to pay medical costs of those who are financially unable to pay.

Net Taxable Estate - The gross estate for federal estate tax purposes reduced by allowable deductions, credits, and charitable contributions.

Non-probate Assets - Assets passing outside the administration of the probate estate. Examples include jointly held assets passing by right of survivorship and life insurance proceeds payable to a named beneficiary.

Payable on Death - A designation for certificates of deposit and bank accounts which states that, upon the owner's death, the account is to be transferred to the named beneficiary.

Per Capita - A method of distributing estate assets so that surviving descendants share equally regardless of generation.

Per Stirpes - A method of distributing estate assets so that the surviving descendants of a predeceased heir will receive only what their immediate ancestor would have received if he or she had been alive at the time of death.

Personal Representative - A person or institution administering an estate, as executor or administrator.

Pour-Over Will - A will used with a revocable living trust that pours over" assets into a trust. Assets controlled by the will must go through probate before it goes into the trust.

Power of Attorney - A document that gives one person (the agent) authority to take legal action and sign the name of another person (the principal).

Pre-Nuptial Agreement - A contract signed by husband and wife before marriage that limits their asset rights in the future.

Principal - The person who signs a power of attorney and thereby gives the agent named therein the authority to act on his or her behalf.

Principal - The assets funding a trust. Trust principal is also known as corpus.

Probate - Procedure which validates a will. It also is used to refer to the administration process of an estate.

Probate Estate - The property and assets of the deceased, distributed under direction of the will.

Probate Assets - The assets that are distributed to heirs under the terms of a will. If there is no will, it passes under the intestacy laws.

Qualified Domestic Trust (Q-DOT) - A trust to which assets are transferred so that a spouse who is not a U.S. citizen will be entitled to claim the benefit of the unlimited marital deduction form the federal estate tax.

Qualified Terminal Interest Property (Q-TIP) Trust - A trust that requires a surviving spouse to receive all income, but which transfers assets to persons designated by the deceased after the death of the surviving spouse. The trust qualifies for the unlimited marital deduction from the federal estate tax.

Remainderman - The person entitled to receive the principal of a trust at the time the prior life estate terminates.

Residue - The portion of an estate that remains after all specific distributions have been made.

Revocable Trust - A trust that can be altered, amended, or revoked by the grantor during lifetime.

Settlor - The grantor or creator of a trust.

Spendthrift Clause - A clause in a trust document that protects assets in a trust from a beneficiary's creditors.

Springing Power of Attorney - A power of attorney that only gives the agent powers after a certain event occurs, such as the incapacity of the principal.

Standby Trust - An unfunded living trust executed with a durable power of attorney to which assets may be subsequently transferred.

Step-Up in Basis - The tax basis of appreciated assets held by a decedent steps up" to fair market value on the date of death.

Successor Trustee - The individual or institution who takes over as trustee of a trust when the original trustee dies, becomes incapacitated, or resigns.

Taxable Estate - The portion of ones estate that is subject to federal and state taxes. Funeral and administrative expenses; debts (including certain unpaid taxes); charitable contributions, and the marital deduction all may be deducted from the gross estate to determine the taxable estate.

Tenancy by Entirety - Joint ownership of assets by husband and wife. Such assets may not be disposed of during life by either spouse without the other's consent. At one spouse's death, the assets are automatically transferred to the survivor.

Tenants-in-Common - A form of joint ownership in which the same assets are owned by two or more persons. At the death of one tenant-in-common, his share is controlled by his will. It does not automatically pass to the surviving tenants-in-common.

Testamentary Trust - A trust that is created under a will and takes effect only after the grantor's death.

Testator or Testatrix (female) - One who has created a will.

Totten Trust - Another term for a pay-on-death bank account.

Trust - A document whereby one individual (called the trustor, grantor or settlor), places assets under the management of another individual or institution (the trustee) for the benefit of a third person (the beneficiary).

Trustee - An individual or institution that administers a trust.

Uniform Transfer to Minors Act - A law that permits one to give a gift to a minor by giving the gift to a custodian who holds title to the assets for the benefit of the minor.

Unlimited Marital Deduction - A provision in the estate and gift tax law that allows a married person to leave unlimited assets to his or her spouse free of gift or estate tax.

Will - A written document with instructions for disposition of assets at death.

Index

U

W

Printed in the United States
39616LVS00006B/121-204